– THE –
ENGLISHMAN
in the Valley

LESLIE J. TUNISON

 FriesenPress

One Printers Way
Altona, MB R0G 0B0
Canada

www.friesenpress.com

ISBN
978-1-03-913753-0 (Hardcover)
978-1-03-913752-3 (Paperback)
978-1-03-913754-7 (eBook)

1. BIOGRAPHY & AUTOBIOGRAPHY, HISTORICAL

Distributed to the trade by The Ingram Book Company

To my mom – for keeping the story alive

and

To my husband – for his encouragement

CONTENTS

PREFACE

SASKATCHEWAN, AND INDEED CANADA, has a rich and diverse population with many remarkable people – some we already know, and some we have yet to meet. This book was written to highlight one of the fascinating and intriguing people from our past. I am certainly not a writer, but felt compelled to tell the story of Aubrey Rooke, as well as a handful of his ancestors. My interest in Aubrey stems from his interactions and relationships with my maternal great-grandfather, grandfather, and mother, whose personal recollections of him have been passed down from one generation to the next.

This book is also the story of the immigrant, having the courage to leave home and begin anew in a different country. In the case of the Rooke family, their roots were in England but the family's branches spread across the globe. They found themselves living among people that did not look like them and who had, from their perspective, strange and unique customs and traditions. And yet they opened themselves up to possibilities and their reward was one of friendship.

Spanning provincial, national, and international borders, this is a story that everyone should learn about. This is a story that had to be told.

I encourage, no, challenge, all of you to look around for stories in your own community. Go out and ask questions. Dig. You never know what you will find and who might be living right next door!

PROLOGUE

GERMANY - 1892
MAKING THE JOURNEY

THE SIGNS WERE EVERYWHERE. "Canada – The Right Land For The Right Man"; "Canada – The New Homeland"; "The Last Best West – Homes For Millions". In Bukovina, Austria, my maternal great-grandfather, Jacob Hellebrand, would have seen posters that read "Kanada – Das Land der Gelegenheit, Berőffentlidht traft der Befugniss, Des Mininsters des Inneren, Ottawa, Kanada", which translated means "Canada – The Country of Opportunity, The Authority is Open to the Public, of the Minister of the Interior, Ottawa, Canada".

As was the case with many Europeans at the time, the Hellebrand family learned of the "New World" through advertisements which encouraged people to leave behind family, friends, and everything familiar to them in order to make a new life. The enticement of a fresh start with limitless opportunities must have been a great pull for young families, who perhaps were struggling to make a living. Jacob and his family answered the call.

In the spring of 1892, Jacob, together with his pregnant wife, Barbara, and three young children, packed up their meager belongings and left their home in Bukovina to make the long journey to Canada, leaving behind the only world they knew, and set off for the unknown.

The Hellebrand family's voyage began in Hamburg, Germany, sailing across the ocean and finally arriving in Canada at Halifax, Nova Scotia, as many had done before them. Making their way across the country, the family found refuge in Winnipeg, Manitoba, with Barbara's cousin, who had made the journey to Canada earlier and had sponsored the family to come.

The baby Barbara had been carrying during the trip was born in May and, only six weeks after the birth, the family was on the move again, travelling further west. The government had promised them a ¼ section of land for $10.00 and they were given two oxen, a wagon, hand plow, bag of flour, and a bag of potatoes. With great hopes, the family started out for their homestead in the area of Fishing Lake, Northwest Territories.

Arriving at their new home, Jacob broke land in the fall. Their first winter was spent in a hole dug into the side of a hill, as was often done, to provide quick shelter for the family. As they settled into the community, and in a desire to fit in with their neighbours, Jacob decided to Anglicize the family name and made the change from Hellebrand to Hildebrand.

The local priest from Lebret, Father Hugonard, heard about the new family in his parish and visited them in the spring. He found them in a dire situation and suggested Jacob go to Lebret and look for work. With his only companion the dog, Jacob walked a distance of 50 miles to town and was fortunate to find employment with the local doctor, Dr. Seymour, driving the horse and buggy in the summer and the sleigh in the winter, taking the doctor on his rounds to visit patients.

THE FRIENDSHIP BEGINS

It was during this time that Jacob became acquainted with an Englishman named Aubrey Rooke. Aubrey was a good friend of Dr. Seymour's and he would often stop in for a visit, also taking the opportunity to call in on Jacob and his family who, by then, had moved to town and were living in a small whitewashed cottage on the doctor's property. These encounters would be the start of a great friendship that would span many decades and live on through three generations of the Hildebrand family.

PART 1:
The Englishman

THE ENGLISHMAN

NEW YEAR'S DAY - 1962
WEYBURN, SASKATCHEWAN

AUBREY ROOKE TOOK HIS final breath in a hospital bed in Weyburn, Saskatchewan, on January 1, 1962. He passed away alone and with little to no financial means. Anyone meeting him would have thought he was just another poor, unfortunate, 85-year-old soul. If only they had known the story of this man's life, they would have realized that assumption could not have been further from the truth. People may have thought there was nothing special about him when, in fact, the opposite was true – there was nothing ordinary about him.

CHRISTMAS EVE - 1876
HAMPSHIRE, ENGLAND

On December 24, 1876, Clement Rooke and his wife, Melissa, were delivered a very special gift – the birth of a son. It was the 4th child the couple were blessed with and they named him Aubrey Murray Rooke. Aubrey joined his siblings: Gertrude (b.1872) and Florence (b.1873). Aubrey's birth was a particular blessing to the couple as their 3rd child,

Russell (b.1875), had survived only two months. One can only imagine the happiness the birth brought to his parents. However, this happiness was short-lived. On February 28, 1877, only two months after Aubrey's birth, his mother, Melissa, passed away at the age of 30.

Aubrey continued to live with his remaining family until he came of school age, at which time he left to attend boarding school at the Royal Asylum of St. Anne's School in Redhill, Reigate, Surrey. His grandfather also lived in Redhill at the time and perhaps that is why this particular school was chosen. His two sisters also left home for boarding school, with the oldest, Gertrude, moving away to attend Christ's Hospital Hertford School for Boys and Girls.

At the age of 16, while at boarding school, Aubrey became seriously ill. Doctors were consulted and he was diagnosed with tuberculosis, being given only a few months to live before he would succumb to the disease. Still a very young man, Aubrey wanted to experience more of the world before he died. His father, Clement, decided Canada would be the best choice to provide his son with the adventure he was seeking, as well as obeying doctors' recommendations of the wide-open spaces and fresh air that were known to improve health. Employment was arranged with the Hudson Bay Company and Aubrey, only 16 years old, left his homeland of England to begin his new life.

Hudson Bay building

1892 - CANADA

Aubrey arrived in Canada in 1892, commencing his employment with the Hudson Bay Company in Winnipeg, Manitoba. He spent the summer there, before being transferred to the post at Fort Qu'Appelle, Saskatchewan. The trading post had been located at Qu'Appelle, Saskatchewan from 1854-1864 before it was re-located to its previous original site at Fort Qu'Appelle. As the population in the area had increased due to the arrival of the settlers, and the bison population was decreasing, the Hudson Bay Company transformed its store from one dedicated to the fur trade to more of a general retail store. In 1897, a new stone and brick building was constructed at the corner of Broadway Street and Company Avenue, where you can still find it today.

WORKING LIFE

Ironically, despite being sent to Canada for its wide-open spaces, Aubrey's life and surroundings in Fort Qu'Appelle were anything but wide open. According to an article in the *Regina Leader-Post* dated December 12, 1940, entitled "A Certain Man Had Two Sons", W.A. Cameron described what life would have been like for Aubrey:

> *Life was hemmed in by the buildings of "the Fort" – the office with the staff sleeping quarters above, the main store and various warehouses – all under the controlling eye of the chief factor, whose dwelling was shut off from the main road by a high board fence once part of the original stockade.*

The article continues, describing the numerous duties Aubrey was expected to perform in his employment:

> *Life for the young clerk was one endless rush from morning till night – now at the office slinging around large journals and ledgers in good old-fashioned style, now at the store counting eggs, weighing butter, unrolling and measuring out dry goods, apron ginghams and shirtings, and serving countless customers with everything from a needle to a*

wagon – and all for the very handsome remuneration of $25 per month, plus $10 for groceries, which had to be purchased from the company.

Aubrey remained at the Hudson Bay Company until 1907 when, after many years of service, he found other employment. He put his talents to good use by going to work at a hardware store in town, where he remained until 1912 when the store burned down. He then found a job at the Elite Café and worked there until 1916 when he joined forces with Jim McDonald in creating McDonald's Meat Market (later known as Saunder's Clothing and Shoes). He retired in 1931.

FIRST NATIONS FRIENDSHIPS

Rooke (left) with Paul Whiteman and family
(Photo Credit: Fort Qu'Appelle Museum)

When Aubrey did have time to look up from his labours, *"there was little to fire the imagination of a boy brought up on Henry and Ballantyne"* (Cameron

– *Regina Leader-Post*, 1940) except for the world of the residents of the local Indian Reserves. *"To the English youth, there was something appealing about them; he was irresistibly drawn to them."* (Cameron – *Regina Leader-Post*, 1940). With Aubrey's natural linguistic abilities, he quickly picked up the languages of Cree and Sioux and was intrigued by the First Nation's rich traditions, culture, and outlook on life. Over a few short years, Aubrey's role transformed from that of a trader and representative of the Crown to a valued advisor to the local First Nations peoples.

As Aubrey settled into life in the community, he became known simply as "Rooke". He had a keen interest in the First Nations people and very quickly became popular with the Sioux of all ages from the nearby Standing Buffalo Reserve. Rooke viewed the Indigenous people as his equal and had an appreciation for their intelligence, with mutual respect being fostered. They would visit back and forth with each other and many friendships developed. The *Winnipeg Free Press* dated June 25, 1927, printed an article by William Bleasdell Cameron entitled "People of Old Fort Qu'Appelle" where Rooke was characterized as follows:

Mr. Rooke is guide, counsellor and friend and, in addition to all this, letter-writer-in-chief to the men and women of Standing Buffalo's band.

An August 18, 1934 *Canadian Press* article appearing in the *Calgary Herald* titled "Naming of Qu'Appelle Legend Is Denied by 64-Year-old Englishman" described Rooke as follows:

Counsellor, adviser, doctor and white chief of the Sioux Indians living on the Qu'Appelle Valley Reserve, the 64-year-old Englishman has lived the life of a near hermit there for 48 years.

A March 17, 1937 article in the *Regina Leader-Post* titled "For Half Century Rooke Counsellor To Valley Indians" expounded further on the close relationship between Rooke and the First Nations people in the Fort Qu'Appelle area. The article declared Rooke:

One of the best known authorities of Indian lore in the Fort Qu'Appelle district.

and called him their "'white chief', counsellor, advisor and friend." The article goes on to note that Rooke was so highly regarded by the First Nations people that he was:

... perhaps the only white man in the district who is welcomed at any and all native celebrations on the reservation.

As an example of this, a portion of the article reads as follows:

Calls on Old Lady:

Following the festivities at the dance, Mr. Rooke went to call on Mrs. John Asham, who is the "grand old lady" of the tribe being 105 years old. She made him tea and was very chatty. Throughout the conversation she smoked her pipe incessantly, her favorite smoking mixture being the manufactured brand mixed with an equal quantity of kinikinick or the bark of the red willow. She lives in a little shack all alone, and her great grandson performs the few chores that she is unable to do herself. She has all her faculties, but her eyesight is not quite as good as it was, and she now complains the smoke somewhat bothers her. She was the wife of Chief John Asham, who predeceased her several years ago.

Rooke was always there to provide assistance and support to his First Nations friends, whether it be financial, emotional, or just help in managing the everyday difficulties of life. His cousin in England described his generosity as living his life "with an open hand". In reciprocation for his aid, and as a sign of friendship, he was given a vast and remarkable collection of First Nations' handicrafts that, at one time, was considered one of the finest in the province. As time went by, however, tourists travelling through the area talked him into selling or giving a majority of these items away.

Rooke, centre, with friends

In 1900, at the age of 24, Rooke was given the rare privilege of being named an honorary chief of the Standing Buffalo Reserve in recognition of his friendship, contribution, and service to the local First Nations people. He was also given the Indigenous name "Khangi Bgoka" (meaning male crow, or "rook").

Rooke standing at gate to his home, Crow's Nest

SPORTS AND COMMUNITY INVOLVEMENT

Rooke, holding trophy (Photo Credit: Fort Qu'Appelle Museum)

Rooke was very involved in developing sports with the youth on the reserve. An achievement he was particularly proud of was the creation of a hockey team comprised of a group of Sioux youth in approximately 1924.

The team travelled to the nearby towns and was very successful, winning several tournaments. Of course, the youth themselves took great pride in their accomplishments as well. He also organized a football team, and brought baseball to the First Nations community. Being a recent immigrant to Canada, Rooke became involved in one of the country's favorite past times – curling. In the years 1900-1901 Rooke joined the Royal Caledonian Curling Club of Scotland, Manitoba Branch, volunteering as the Secretary-Treasurer for the Fort Qu'Appelle Club. He shared his passion for the sport with the First Nations people, getting them involved as well.

FORT SAN AND DR. SEYMOUR

Dr. Maurice Seymour (Photo Credit: Provincial Archives of Saskatchewan R-A5569)

Dr. Maurice Seymour, born in Goderich, Ontario, and educated at McGill University in Montreal, was a physician and surgeon who moved out to Winnipeg and then on to Fort Qu'Appelle to continue his medical career. He had a general practice in Fort Qu'Appelle from 1885-1904 and, during this time, also headed the Medical Council of the Northwest Territories. In addition, it was under Dr. Seymour's leadership as Commissioner of Public Health for the province that the Saskatchewan Medical Association was established in 1906.

One of the primary areas of interest and expertise in Dr. Seymour's career was tuberculosis. He treated patients in his home until 1912 when, as the founder of the Saskatchewan Anti-Tuberculosis League, he became instrumental in the construction of the Sanatorium (commonly referred to as "the San"). The San operated between 1912 and 1971, becoming the main treatment centre for tuberculosis in the Province of Saskatchewan, with a capacity of 350 patients.

Given that both Dr. Seymour and Rooke had a common interest in tuberculosis – one as a doctor and one as a patient – perhaps that was what initially brought the two men together. It may even have been possible that Dr. Seymour treated Rooke and their friendship grew from that association.

As the reason for Rooke's emigration to Canada was the diagnosis of tuberculosis, he had an affinity for the patients sent to the San for treatment and a personal knowledge of what they were experiencing. He would often be seen visiting his First Nations friends, as described in an article in the *Regina Leader-Post* dated December 12, 1940, by W.A. Cameron:

> *Visit the Indian hospital or the "San" at Fort Qu'Appelle, and you will find him there going his unofficial rounds from room to room, chatting, comforting and cheering his adopted people.*

DISPUTING THE NAMING OF QU'APPELLE

In a *Canadian Press* newspaper article *"Naming of Qu'Appelle Legend Is Denied by 64-Year-old Englishman"* printed in the *Calgary Herald* on August 18, 1934, Rooke was consulted by the reporter to provide his opinion as to the legend of the naming of Fort Qu'Appelle. The poem by Pauline Johnson talks of a young man calling for his mate, with Qu'Appelle meaning "who calls". Having lived in the area for over 40 years by that time, Rooke disputed this definition of the word "Qu'Appelle" and had his own interpretation:

> *The first church in the valley was a Catholic one called 'La Chappelle'. The word Qu'Appelle comes from the French Chappelle.*

LIFE IN THE COMMUNITY

Rooke was a very friendly, outgoing gentleman who would greet all who passed him on the street. He was particularly fond of young children and would often entertain them by performing various coin tricks. Due to the close relationship between Rooke and my mother's family, he was a frequent visitor to their home. My mother has very fond memories of him from her childhood and always found it remarkable that even though she was just a child, he would stop to say hello and spend some time with her. On one occasion she recalls sitting under a tree with him while he tried to teach her sign language.

Rooke was also godfather to my mother's cousins and she remembers hearing this story from one of them:

> *When Rooke was a clerk at the Hudson Bay store, my cousin would go peek in the window and stare at him until he saw her. He would call her in and give her some candy. She would grab it like a starving waif and run.*

This would have been in the 1930s when the family was experiencing hard times. Often the family did not have anything to eat and one of the cousins recalled the extent of the desperation. She remembers once:

> ... *following a grocer to the dump where I saw him throw out some spoiled apples. I ran home, got a knife, cut away all the rot and ate until I was sick.*

My mother was told of another instance when one of her young cousins would visit Rooke:

> ... *he would give her an orange if she'd dance for him. Of course she wouldn't, but she did think about it. The next time she saw him, she did tap her toe back and forth a couple of times and he gave her the orange.*

He was a kind and generous man who had a particular empathy and compassion for people less fortunate than himself.

PAPER RAILWAY BARON

Considering the importance of the railway in settling western Canada, the Canadian government implemented a policy in the early 1880s of providing land grants or subsidies to facilitate the construction of branch railways which would encourage homesteaders to the prairies.

As the population in Fort Qu'Appelle was growing, a branch line running through the community would have been greatly desirable for the transport of goods and services, for travel, and to assist farmers in hauling their grain out of the valley to market. With the arrival of a rail line, various other commodities such as cream and hogs could be produced as access to the markets would then have been possible. The railways also used their own telegraph system to provide a telegram service to the community, allowing the residents to send and receive messages.

Every proposed route for a railway was contentious and every town and village wanted to be on the rail line. It seems that Fort Qu'Appelle was no exception.

On April 29, 1901, during the Ninth Parliament of the Dominion of Canada, a debate was held in the House of Commons regarding the granting of a charter to the Canadian Pacific Railway to construct a rail line in the neighbouring district of Manitoba. The MP for Assiniboia West, Mr. Walter Scott (who later became Saskatchewan's First Premier), argued that before this charter was granted in Manitoba, the Railway should be obliged to first construct a branch line through the district of the Qu'Appelle Valley:

MR. SCOTT: I ask that this charter should not be granted to the Canadian Pacific Railway Company until they agree to certain conditions which, I contend, are manifestly in the interest of a certain portion of the people of Canada – a large number of the people of the North-west Territories.

…

Almost twenty years ago a large number of settlers went into the country north of the Qu'Appelle valley. These people, in the North-west, are strung along from the Manitoba boundary to Long Lake, north of Regina. FORT QU'APPELLE IS IN THAT DISTRICT. (author's emphasis) Year after year since the Canadian Pacific Railway acquired the North-west Central charter, delegates representing the people in that country have gone to Winnipeg and have endeavoured to prevail upon the Canadian Pacific Railway Company to extend the road and give them the railway communication they need. And year after year, the representatives of the Canadian Pacific Railway have represented to these people that the company was financially unable to extend the line.

…

... but they say that the people in that district will have to exercise patience until the company becomes financially able to construct the road.

[Official Report of the Debates of the House of Commons of the Dominion of Canada, First Session-Ninth Parliament, 1 Edward VII, 1901, (p.3986)]

Mr. Scott continued his argument in support of the residents' attempts to gain a railway line through the Fort Qu'Appelle area as follows:

MR. SCOTT: It was, I think, three years ago this last winter that, travelling westward from Winnipeg, I met gentlemen on the train who were delegates and had been down to Winnipeg to interview the Canadian Pacific Railway officials.... They met Mr. Whyte, the general manager, and other representatives of the Canadian Pacific Railway Company in Winnipeg, and placed the case before them as I have stated it. These representatives of the company said that the company would build the road into that country as soon as it was able to do so. It seems to me an entirely reasonable proposition that, when the company come here and ask power to construct 100 miles of road into a portion of the country where there are few people and where, so far as I am aware, there is no person particularly anxious to have the road built, WE SHOULD MAKE IT CONDITIONAL UPON THE GRANTING OF THIS CHARTER THAT THE COMPANY SHOULD SPEND THEIR MONEY FIRST IN THE PORTION OF THE COUNTRY WHERE RAILWAY COMMUNICATION IS VERY URGENTLY NEEDED. (author's emphasis).

[Official Report of the Debates of the House of Commons of the Dominion of Canada, First Session-Ninth Parliament, 1 Edward VII, 1901, (p.3986)]

Mr. Scott also addressed the farmers' need for a rail line through the valley:

MR. SCOTT:… in the district through which the projected North-west Central line runs, there is a production of wheat amounting to about half a million bushels a year. There is something like 50,000 acres of land under cultivation there, and there are many settlers. All that wheat, or the greater part of it, has to be transported an average distance of 25 or 30 miles. That is not the worst of it, the wheat has to be transported across the Qu'Appelle Valley, the banks of which are 240 or 250 feet high. So I say that even if we are creating a precedent in this matter, it is a very good precedent to create.

[Official Report of the Debates of the House of Commons of the Dominion of Canada, First Session-Ninth Parliament, 1 Edward VII, 1901, (p.3986)]

The argument continued back and forth in the House that every community in the Dominion of Canada wanted a railway running through their town; it was impossible to accommodate all requests; and, it would be unfair to favour one community over another. In addition, it would be setting a poor precedent for the government to "coerce" the CPR into doing its bidding in exchange for granting the charter they were requesting.

In the end, after all the debating was over, the CPR was granted their charter request for Manitoba, without any conditions attached.

During the same session of Parliament, certain Government Acts were passed, one being an Act to incorporate a company called "The Fort Qu'Appelle Railway Company". This Act was the result of a petition made to the government by a group of leading businessmen from the community. Aubrey Rooke was among the men who made the application.

The petition filed by Rooke and his partners was tabled in the Senate as a Private Bill on March 6, 1901, and had its first reading March 8. The mandate for the formation of the company was to:

#8... lay out, construct, and operate a... railway of the gauge of four feet eight and one-half inches from a point in or near McLean station or Qu'Appelle station or Indian Head station on the Canadian Pacific Railway to a point in or near the Village of Qu'Appelle, otherwise known as Fort Qu'Appelle, in the district of Assiniboia, in the Northwest Territories.

[Acts of the Parliament of the Dominion of Canada, 1
Edward VII, May 23, 1901, Chap. 58, (p.58)]

The Bill was granted Royal Assent and passed into law on May 23, 1901, providing the Fort Qu'Appelle Railway Company with a very desirable government charter.

ACTS

OF THE

PARLIAMENT

OF THE

DOMINION OF CANADA

PASSED IN THE SESSION HELD IN THE

FIRST YEAR OF THE REIGN OF HIS MAJESTY

KING EDWARD VII.

BEING THE

FIRST SESSION OF THE NINTH PARLIAMENT

Begun and holden at Ottawa, on the Sixth day of February, and closed by Prorogation on the Twenty-third day of May, 1901

HIS EXCELLENCY THE

RIGHT HONOURABLE SIR GILBERT JOHN ELLIOT, EARL OF MINTO

GOVERNOR GENERAL

VOL II.

LOCAL AND PRIVATE ACTS

OTTAWA

PRINTED BY SAMUEL EDWARD DAWSON

LAW PRINTER TO THE KING'S MOST EXCELLENT MAJESTY

ANNO DOMINI 1901

1 EDWARD VII.

CHAP. 58.

An Act to incorporate the Fort Qu'Appelle Railway Company.

[*Assented to 23rd May*, 1901.]

WHEREAS a petition has been presented praying that it be **Preamble.** enacted as hereinafter set forth, and it is expedient to grant the prayer of the said petition : Therefore His Majesty, by and with the advice and consent of the Senate and House of Commons of Canada, declares and enacts as follows :—

1. Cuthbert Lionel Fetherstonhaugh, Robert Williams, **Incorpora-** Henry Hawkesworth Hayward, William Hall, John Mc-**tion.** Lellan, Aubrey Murray Rooke, John Malcolm Boyles, Frederick Stephen Proctor, Donald Hogarth McDonald, James Dillon, Thomas Edward Baker and Charles Payne, all of the village of Qu'Appelle, in the North-west Territories, together with such persons as become shareholders in the company, are incorporated under the name of "The Fort Qu'Appelle **Corporate** Railway Company," hereinafter called "the Company." **name.**

2. The undertaking of the Company is declared to be a **Declaratory.** work for the general advantage of Canada.

3. The persons named in section 1 of this Act are consti-**Provisional** tuted provisional directors of the Company. **directors.**

4. The capital stock of the Company shall be two hundred **Capital stock.** thousand dollars and may be called up by the directors from time to time as they deem necessary, but no one call shall exceed ten per cent on the shares subscribed.

5. The head office of the Company shall be in the village **Head office.** of Qu'Appelle, Assiniboia.

6. The annual meeting of the shareholders shall be held on **Annual** the first day of September in each year. **meeting.**

57   **7.**

26

2   Chap. 58.   *Fort Qu'Appelle Railway Co.*   1 EDW. VII.

Election of directors.

7. At such meeting the subscribers for the capital stock assembled who have paid all calls due on their shares shall choose seven persons to be directors of the Company, one or more of whom may be paid directors.

Line of railway described.

8. The Company may lay out, construct and operate an electric railway of the gauge of four feet eight and one-half inches from a point in or near McLean station or Qu'Appelle station or Indian Head station on the Canadian Pacific Railway to a point in or near the village of Qu'Appelle, otherwise known as Fort Qu'Appelle, in the district of Assiniboia, in the North-west Territories.

Bond issue.

9. The Company may issue bonds, debentures or other securities to the extent of twenty thousand dollars per mile of the railway, and such bonds, debentures or other securities may be issued only in proportion to the length of railway constructed or under contract to be constructed.

Telegraph and telephone lines.

10. The Company may construct and operate telegraph and telephone lines along the whole length of its railway and branches, and may establish offices for the transmission of messages for the public and collect tolls for so doing; and for the purposes of operating such telegraph and telephone lines, the Company may enter into a contract with any other company, or may lease the Company's lines or any part thereof; and may connect its lines with the lines of any telegraph or telephone company.

Agreement with telegraph or telephone company.

2. The Company may enter into arrangements with any telegraph or telephone company for the exchange or transmission of messages, or for the working in whole or in part of the lines of the Company.

Rates to be approved.

3. No rates or charges shall be demanded or taken from any person for the transmission of any message by telegraph or telephone or for leasing or using the telegraphs or telephones of the Company, until such rates or charges have been approved by the Governor in Council, and such rates and charges shall be subject to revision, from time to time, by the Governor in Council.

R.S.C., c. 132.

4. *The Electric Telegraph Companies Act* shall apply to the telegraphic business of the Company.

Powers.

11. The Company may, in connection with its railway and for the purposes of its business,

Motive power.

(*a.*) acquire lands and erect, use and manage works and manufacture machinery and plant for the generation, transmission and distribution of electric power and energy and other motive power;

Docks, warehouses, etc.

(*b.*) acquire land for wharfs, docks, elevators, warehouses and coal-bunkers in connection with the operations of the Company and erect buildings thereon, and collect wharfage and storage charges for the use thereof;

(*c.*)

27

(*c.*) acquire exclusive rights in letters patent, franchises or Patent rights. patent rights for the purpose of the works and undertakings hereby authorized, and again dispose of such rights ;

(*d.*) sell or lease any surplus power which it may develop or Surplus power. acquire, either as water power or other motive power, or by converting the same into electricity or other force for the distribution of light, heat or power or for all purposes for which electricity or other motive power can be used, with power to transmit the same ;

(*e.*) subject to such regulations as may be imposed by the Water for works. Governor in Council, acquire and dispose of lands and construct, acquire and dispose of buildings and other erections and plant for the purpose of supplying water for the use of its works and railway.

12. If the Company requires land for wharfs, docks, ware- Expropriation of lands. houses, elevators or bunkers, and cannot agree for the purchase thereof with the owner of such land, it may cause a map or plan and book of reference to be made of such land, and all the provisions of sections 107 to 111, both inclusive, of *The* 1888, c. 29. *Railway Act*, shall apply to the subject matter of this section and to the obtaining of such land and to determining the compensation therefor.

13. The Company may enter into an agreement with the Agreement with another company. Canadian Pacific Railway Company for conveying or leasing to such company the railway of the Company, in whole or in part, or any rights or powers acquired under this Act, as also the franchises, surveys, plans, works, plant, material, machinery and other property to it belonging, or for an amalgamation with such company, on such terms and conditions as are agreed upon, and subject to such restrictions as to the directors seem fit ; provided that such agreement has been first ap- Approval of shareholders and Governor in Council. proved by two-thirds of the votes at a special general meeting of the shareholders duly called for the purpose of considering it, at which meeting shareholders representing at least two-thirds in value of the stock are present or represented by proxy, and that such agreement has also received the sanction of the Governor in Council.

2. Such sanction shall not be signified until after notice of Notice of application for sanction. the proposed application therefor has been published in the manner and for the time set forth in section 239 of *The Railway Act*, and also for a like period in one newspaper in each of the counties or electoral districts through which the railway of the Company runs, and in which a newspaper is published.

3. A duplicate of the agreement referred to in subsection Agreement to be filed with Secretary of State. **1** of this section shall, within thirty days after its execution, be filed in the office of the Secretary of State of Canada, and notice thereof shall be given by the Company in *The Canada*

59   *Gazette,*

Gazette, and the production of *The Canada Gazette* containing such notice shall be prima facie evidence of the requirements of this section having been complied with.

OTTAWA : Printed by Samuel Edward Dawson, Law Printer to the King's most Excellent Majesty.

1 EDWARD VII.

CHAP. 59.

An Act to amend an Act passed during the present Session, intituled "An Act to incorporate the Fort Qu'Appelle Railway Company."

[Assented to 23rd May, 1901.]

HIS Majesty, by and with the advice and consent of the Senate and House of Commons of Canada, enacts as follows :—

1. Section 8 of the Act passed during the present session of Parliament and intituled *An Act to incorporate the Fort Qu'Appelle Railway Company* is amended by substituting for the words "an electric railway," in the first and second lines thereof, the words "a railway." Section 8 amended.

OTTAWA : Printed by SAMUEL EDWARD DAWSON, Law Printer to the King's most Excellent Majesty.

61

[Acts of the Parliament of the Dominion of Canada, 1 Edward VII, May 23, 1901, Chap. 58]

Once a charter was granted to a company, investors were required to fund the project. While the Government did provide subsidies and land grants, these were only paid out when the railway was completed and operating. In the interim, financing would be needed. While local people in the community would have been invited to buy into the company as shareholders, foreign investors (mostly in Europe) would also be recruited. Most shareholders would have joined the venture hoping to reap a large financial reward, not to actually operate the railway. As such, once the track was built, the object would have been to lease the track to an existing company (Canadian Pacific, Canadian Northern, or the Grand Trunk Pacific) or sell it outright to another company.

Selling shares in the company was the most advantageous method for the directors to raise funds as they would maintain control of the company. However, the issuance of bonds was another avenue that the necessary capital could be achieved, with interest being paid to the bond-holder when the bonds expired.

FAILURE OF THE RAIL LINE

The plan proposed by Rooke and his fellow directors was to construct a branch line that would run north off of the existing Canadian Pacific mainline. Building this line, however, would have been a monumental task as no clear route was available through the coulees and hills of this rugged terrain. Complicating matters was that the route into the valley from this direction would have required excavating a great deal of earth to create a reasonable grade, making this project economically unfeasible.

Consequently, despite the fact that the Fort Qu'Appelle Railway Company had obtained a charter from the Dominion of Canada, and a coalition of directors was in place, no track was ever laid. Thus, the project is referred to as a "paper railway". While hundreds of railway charters were granted, many, if not most, of these lines were never constructed. The task of constructing a railway would have been an immense undertaking with numerous obstacles to overcome.

A railway through Fort Qu'Appelle was eventually laid in 1911 by the Grand Trunk Pacific (now known as Canadian National) that ran from Melville to Regina. This route succeeded as the terrain was less rugged and was more conducive to laying track.

While the goal of the Fort Qu'Appelle Railway Company did not succeed, it is remarkable that Rooke was considered one of the leaders of the community involved in such a huge venture. He was 25 years old.

Rooke, age 21 (Photo Credit: Fort Qu'Appelle Museum)

POLLING STATION – ELECTION 1904

Rooke, seated in chair, centre; Dominion election polling station at
Crow's Nest, Nov. 3, 1904
(Photo Credit: Provincial Archives of Saskatchewan R-B1776)

Between 1871 and 1921 Canada's population more than doubled, from 4 million to over 8.5 million largely due to immigration. The largest increase in population was in the prairie provinces, increasing from 75,000 to almost 2 million. In the middle of the boom, a Federal election was called asking the residents of the country to cast their votes. Of course, Rooke stepped up and volunteered to help.

The election was held for the Dominion of Canada on November 3, 1904. At the time, the Fort Qu'Appelle district was considered part of the "Qu'Appelle Riding", which also included the North West Territories. A year later, in 1905, after Saskatchewan became a province, the riding was amended to cover only Saskatchewan. The Member of Parliament for the area was the Conservative Party member, Richard Stuart Lake, who later became the province's third Lieutenant Governor. That same year, Wilfred Laurier won his third term as Prime Minister, beating the Conservative Party led by Robert Borden.

The location of polling stations was at the direction of the Returning Officer of the riding – in this case, Mr. Frederick B. Lewis, a farmer and resident of Wolseley. While we currently are accustomed to polling stations being located in school gyms, libraries, and church basements, these facilities may not have been available in small communities back in 1904. Often they would be found in private homes – in a front hall or living room. Wishing to be of assistance to his fellow residents, Rooke agreed to have a polling station situated on his property and a tent was erected to facilitate the vote. While the use of a tent would have been unusual, it may have been more common on the sparsely populated prairies than elsewhere.

The determination and regulations as to the location for polling stations in a federal election are as follows:

51. The poll shall be held in each polling division in a room or building of convenient access, with an outside door for the admittance of voters, and having, if possible, another door through which they may leave after having voted; and one or two compartments shall be made within the room, so arranged that each voter may be screened from observation, and may, without interference or interruption, mark his ballot paper; and a table or desk with a hard and smooth surface shall be provided, upon which the voter may mark his ballot paper; and a suitable black lead pencil shall be provided and kept properly sharpened throughout the hours of polling for the use of the voters in marking their ballots.

[Dominion Elections Act, 1900 (S.C. 1900, c. 12) (s.51) (p.102)]

A small fee would have been provided to the individual who granted access to their home and property for the polling station location:

19. For use, when a public building is not obtainable, of private buildings for nomination, outlay, not exceeding four dollars.

[Dominion Elections Act, 1900 (S.C. 1900, c.12) (s.147), (para. 19), (p.154)]

Also, any costs that would have been incurred by the individual was stipulated:

27. Actual expenses incurred for the use of polling stations, not exceeding ten dollars in cities, or four dollars in other electoral districts, - this fee to cover fuel, light and furniture.

[Dominion Elections Act, 1900 (S.C. 1900, c.12) (s.147), (para. 27), (p.154)]

Considering Rooke's generous nature and sense of community, his volunteering the use of his land for the location of the polling station would not have come as a surprise.

THE HAWAIIAN TALE

Rooke entered into the orbit of my family from a relationship that developed between my maternal great-grandfather, Jacob Hellebrand, and their mutual friend, Dr. Seymour. As Jacob's family continued to grow with more children being born, so did the relationship between Rooke and the family. One of those children was my grandfather, Joseph (Joe) Hildebrand. Rooke was a frequent visitor at the family home and a strong friendship developed between Joe and Rooke, despite their age difference of 24 years.

Rooke's home in the Fort Qu'Appelle valley became known as "Crow's Nest" and was a very popular gathering spot for the young men in the community, including my grandfather Joe. To them, Rooke was just one of the guys – an interesting, eccentric Englishman to hang out with. While Rooke lived a simple and unassuming life in small shack in the valley, no one would ever have guessed what a distinguished and important family he had come from, including being related to the queen of Hawaii.

Rooke, front row, left. My grandfather with cap

When my mother was young, my grandfather would often tell her an amazing story of his travelling with Rooke to claim an inheritance from relatives in Hawaii who were part of the Hawaiian Royal Family. Mother never really knew whether grandfather was telling the truth or if he was just telling a tall tale to entertain her. As unbelievable as the story would have seemed to a young girl in the 1940s living on a farm in southern Saskatchewan, the story was true.

ROYAL CONNECTION

A distance of over 3,500 miles separates Fort Qu'Appelle from Hawaii and the locations could not be more dissimilar. However, each of the two destinations had one thing in common: a member of the Rooke family.

While Rooke had left England at a very young age to begin a new life in Canada, he was not the first member of the family who had chosen such a path. Several decades earlier, in 1829, history reveals another member of the Rooke family making the same decision to leave his birthplace for another country far away. Rooke's great-uncle, Dr. Thomas Charles Byde Rooke, had also departed his homeland of England, travelling as a young man to the Hawaiian Islands to live out his days.

As was the case with Rooke, who settled in his new country and developed strong relationships and friendships with the Chiefs and Indigenous people, so it was with his great-uncle, Dr. Rooke. While Rooke never knew his great-uncle (Dr. Rooke died before Rooke was born), both men shared a great love, admiration, appreciation, and respect for the Indigenous people of their new homeland. The striking difference between the two men was that while Rooke lived a very understated, meager life, near poverty in a shack in the hills of a small town in the Canadian prairies, Dr. Rooke lived a life of wealth, prestige, and affluence among the Chiefs of the Hawaiian Royal Family during the Kamehameha Dynasty.

It is through Rooke's family connection to Dr. T.C.B. Rooke that an inheritance of Hawaiian property was to be his.

THE LEGACY

The story of Rooke's Hawaiian inheritance was indeed true. Back home in England, Rooke's uncle, Colonel Cresswell Rooke, had fought for and won ownership of numerous parcels of land previously owned by Dr. T.C.B. Rooke. (This will be discussed later in greater detail.) As Colonel Rooke was organizing his legal affairs, he had prepared his Last Will and Testament making Rooke one of his beneficiaries. The relevant portion of the Will read (with no punctuation in the document):

Should all my children die without issue then I bequeath the whole of my estate to my half brother Benjamin Procter Simpson Rooke absolutely failing his inheriting then to his children in equal shares absolutely should no child of the said Benjamin Procter Simpson Rooke be living then to my nephew Aubrey Murray Rooke absolutely.

In 1927, Rooke received notification of this inheritance of property located in Hawaii. My mother recalls: *"I remember my dad said he had seen these documents and they had looked very official, with red seals all over them and a blue ribbon at the top."*

PLANNING FOR THE TRIP

The trip from Fort Qu'Appelle to Hawaii to claim the inheritance would have required extensive arrangements and planning in preparation for the great journey. For whatever reason, Rooke decided he must travel to Hawaii as a proper English gentleman would. And what does a proper English gentleman require during his travels? A personal valet, of course. He considered among all of his friends and acquaintances who would be the best candidate to fulfill this important role and chose my grandfather to join him on this wild adventure. He could not have made a better choice. Grandfather was always eager, willing, and able to participate in a bit of fun and agreed to play the role of valet in the charade. Somehow Rooke found a book that described the duties and requirements of a valet and gave it to grandfather to study and learn what his role would be. Being born and raised in small town Saskatchewan, and living a very simple and modest life as a farmer, one can only imagine how unbelievable it would have seemed to my grandfather to even think about travelling to a distant land such as Hawaii. However, given his easy-going, jovial nature, I am sure he would have thought it would be quite a lark.

THE ADVENTURE BEGINS

And so the grand adventure began, with the 52-year-old Englishman travelling in style with his 28-year-old personal valet by his side. They boarded the train in Fort Qu'Appelle and headed west on the CN rail line, through the Rocky Mountains, and on to Prince Rupert, British Columbia.

Along the way, my grandfather picked up a few postcards and documented the journey on the backs of the cards. Postcards #1-#3 describe the beginning of the trip through the Rocky Mountains, to Prince Rupert, and their plans to travel to Vancouver by boat.

Postcard #1 dated January 26, 1928, describes the first leg of their trip as far as Prince Rupert:

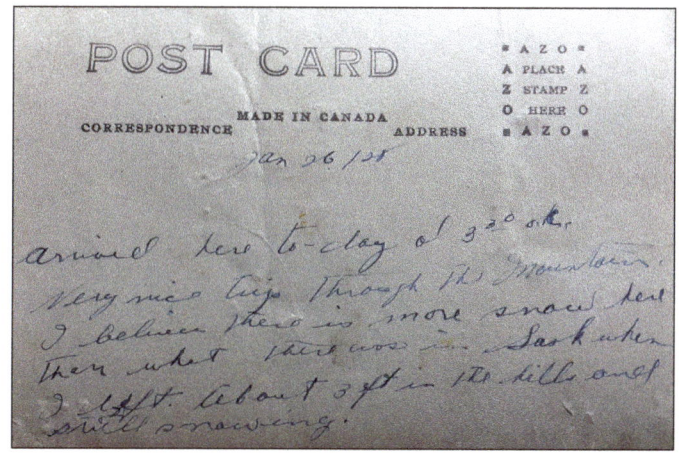

January 26, 1928

Arrived here today at 3:30 o'clock. Very nice trip through the mountains. I believe there is more snow here than what there was in Sask when I left. About 3 ft in the hills and still snowing.

Postcard #2 continues from Prince Rupert:

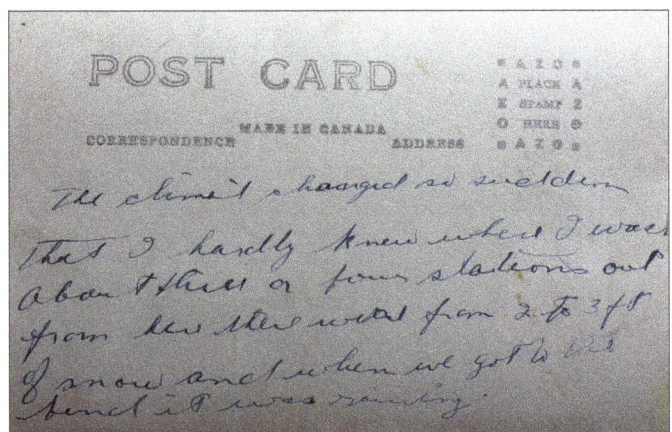

The climate changed so sudden that I hardly knew where I was. About three or four stations out from here there went from 2 to 3 ft of snow and when we got to the bend it was raining.

He writes on Postcard #3 from Mt. Robson Park:

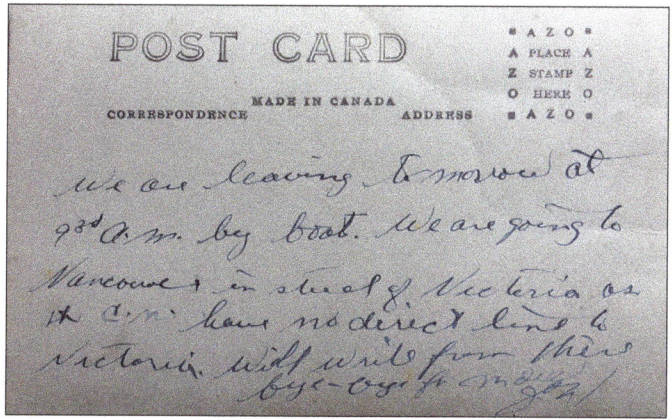

We are leaving tomorrow at 9:30 a.m. by boat. We are going to Vancouver instead of Victoria as the C.N. have no direct line to Victoria. Will write from there bye-bye for now. Joe

By Postcard #4 they had made it across the Canadian/American border and were now in Seattle, Washington. It sounds like it was a whirl-wind trip. As the card indicates, the next stop was Honolulu:

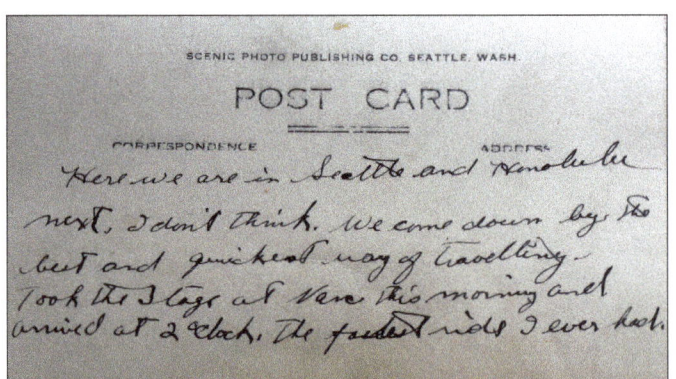

Here we are in Seattle and Honolulu next. I don't think we came down by the best and quickest way of travelling. Took the stage at Vanc this morning and arrived at 2 o'clock. The fastest ride I ever had.

Once in Seattle, the plan was to board a ship and head to Hawaii. However, difficulties arose at the U.S. Customs. My mother recalls the story as follows:

The U.S. Border Agent proceeded to ask the usual questions: Where are you going? How long are you going to be away? What is the purpose of your trip? Hearing Rooke's story about the inheritance, the fellow at Customs said he could not inherit any property from the Hawaiian Islands unless he was an American citizen. Rooke asked what he had to do to become an American citizen and the man said he would have to live in the United States for five years and give up his British citizenship. Of course, being a staunch Englishman, Rooke would never do that and told the fellow he could go to heck.

With that decision, Rooke lost his shot at the inheritance of property and the wealth that would have come with it. He must not have been too disappointed, however, because he and grandfather proceeded to take advantage of the opportunity to do some sightseeing on the West Coast, travelling first to Portland, Oregon, and then over to Victoria, B.C.

In Postcard #5 my grandfather writes to his uncle, Walter, while in Portland:

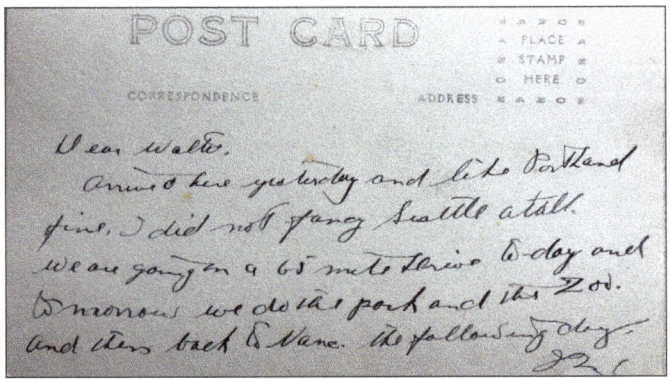

Dear Walter,

Arrived here yesterday and like Portland fine. I did not fancy Seattle at all. We are going on a 65 mile drive to-day and tomorrow we do the park and the zoo and then back to Vanc. the following day.

Joe

From what my grandfather writes on Postcard #6, it sounds like they had quite an interesting time while in Victoria:

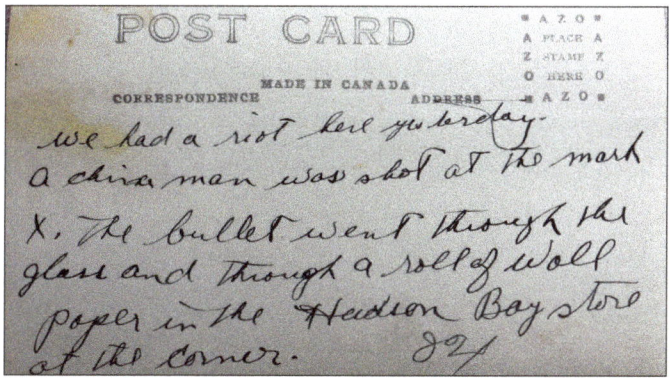

We had a riot here yesterday. A china man was shot at the mark X. The bullet went through the glass and through a roll of wall paper in the Hudson Bay store at the corner.

Joe

(You can see the X mark on the far left corner of the picture.)

From Victoria, they made their way home.

So, while Rooke had the opportunity to fulfill the dream of a lifetime that a lot of people have – one of being left an inheritance of property in the Hawaiian Islands and becoming wealthy – to him, it was not worth giving up his British heritage and changing who he was. Still, what an exciting adventure they had. A trip of a lifetime – and what a story it would make when they got back home.

TRACKING ROOKE

During Rooke's life in Canada, he often shared accommodations with others. In the 1901 Canadian Census, eight years after his arrival in the country, he is shown in Fort Qu'Appelle at the age of 24 living as a lodger with the Boyles family (Mr. Boyles is listed as a hotel keeper). His occupation is that of a clerk.

By 1906, Rooke, at the age of 31, appears in the Census as having his own place and living on his own.

The Census of 1911 reveals Aubrey as the head of the house, with an occupation described as "Retail Merchant". The Payne family is living with him at this time: Alfred (carpenter); wife, Mildred; and, their two girls Geraldine (2 years old) and Alva (11 months old).

Five years later, in 1916, Rooke is referred to as an accountant in a grocery store. He is listed as a lodger once again, this time living with a couple who had also emigrated from England, being the Greatorex family: Ernest (bookkeeper at an implement store); wife, Edith; and, their young son Jeoffrey (3 years old).

By 1921, Rooke, now 46 years old, is still living with the Greatorex family as a lodger, employed at a grocery store, and listed as a clerk.

The 1926 Census shows Rooke listed as 52 years old, living by himself. There is no column for occupation on this Census form.

In 1940, Rooke is still living in Fort Qu'Appelle and is listed in the Voters List with an occupation being that of a "farmer". (He had retired in 1931.)

The 1945 Voters List records Rooke residing in Fort Qu'Appelle, and he is described as a "gentleman". He is now aged 69.

By age 73, in 1949, Rooke had left Fort Qu'Appelle and made the move to the city. He had taken up residence in Regina at 828 Victoria Avenue, sharing accommodations with John Sutter (carpenter); his wife Dorothy; and, a widow named Anne Morrison. He is listed as being "retired".

In 1953, Rooke moved once again, just up the street from his former residence. The Voters List has him now at 2932 Victoria Avenue, Regina, living with two couples: Mr. Victor Ing (café); his wife, Mrs. Chow Ing; and, Mr. S.H. Deeks (farmer) and his wife Evelyn. At this time he was 77 years old.

Four years later, in 1957, Rooke is no longer listed in the home. The Deeks couple is still there, as well as the Ing family, now describing Victor Ing as (proprietor); Mrs. Joan Ing; Miss Kay Ing (Civil Servant); and, Roger Ing (waiter). Rooke was now 81 years old.

In about 1953, my mother recalls driving with my grandparents to Regina to pick Rooke up and take him to St. Anthony's nursing home in Moose Jaw. Grandfather walked up to the house to get him. All Rooke had with him was a small satchel containing his personal belongings – presumably toiletries, a change of clothing and some pajamas. They dropped him off at the home. At some point he must have developed dementia as he was sent to Weyburn Mental Hospital, where he eventually died in 1962.

Aubrey Rooke, a man who turned down a fortune in land in Hawaii, lived his life as a pauper and passed away with little or no financial means. Through the years, two of his family members had offered financial support, however he had refused to even consider it. In the end, his long-time friends, the Greatorex family, paid for his headstone located in the Lakeview Cemetery on Fort Qu'Appelle's south hill. One would suspect he would not have had it any other way.

Headstone of Aubrey Rooke

Mac Anderson on horseback, Rooke in cart
(Photo Credit: Fort Qu'Appelle Museum)

l. to r. Unidentified, Rooke, Dr. Seymour

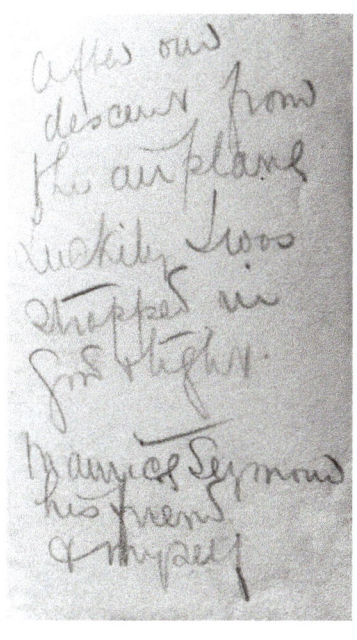

Rooke's handwriting on back of photo: "After our descent from the airplane. Luckily I was strapped in good & tight. Maurice Seymour, his friend & myself."

l. to r. Rooke, Unidentified

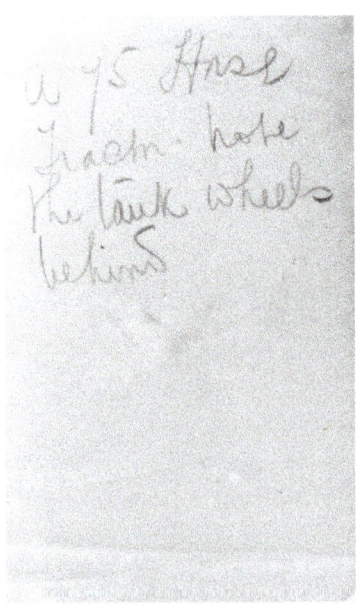

Rooke's handwriting on back of photo: "A 75 horse tractor. Note the tank wheels behind"

Halbgewach/Huber wedding party at Sioux Flats
l. to r. Clara Spanier, Rooke, Rosie Huber
(Photo Credit: Provincial Archives of Saskatchewan R-B1934)

Rooke standing outside Crow's Nest

Crow's Nest (Photo Credit: Provincial Archives of Saskatchewan R-A6510)

Street sign in Fort Qu'Appelle

PART 2:
The Family

Delving deeper into Aubrey Rooke's personal history uncovered a treasure trove of fascinating people in his family line. The following section of the book describes the extraordinary lives of a few of his predecessors and the familial relationship to Aubrey.

Benjamin Rooke

(1742-1823) – (Great-Great-Grandfather)

BENJAMIN ROOKE

SERVICE TO THE COMMUNITY began generations earlier in the Rooke family with Aubrey Rooke's great-great-grandfather Benjamin Rooke, born 1742 in Hertfordshire, England. Benjamin sat on the Hertford town council as an Alderman for 27 years and became Mayor in 1797. He was an attorney by profession.

Benjamin Rooke (Photo Credit: Hertford Town Council)

THOMAS WILDMAN ROOKE

(1769-1814) – (Great-Grandfather)

THOMAS WILDMAN ROOKE

THOMAS WILDMAN ROOKE WAS born in Bengeo, Hertfordshire, in 1769 to Benjamin Rooke and his wife Anna Maria Wildman. He would go on to marry Sarah Paillet Draper on February 20, 1800, and father two sons who would each have a special connection to Queen Victoria of England: Benjamin Proctor Rooke (b.1801) and Thomas Charles Byde Rooke (b.1806). Unfortunately, Thomas would not live to see the great accomplishments of his sons as he died on February 21, 1814, when Benjamin and Thomas were just 13 and 8 years old respectively.

Benjamin Proctor Rooke

(1801-1887) – (Grandfather)

BENJAMIN PROCTOR ROOKE

BORN MAY 5, 1801, in Bengeo, Hertfordshire, Benjamin Proctor Rooke was the son of Thomas Rooke and Sarah Paillet Draper. As was the case with other members of the Rooke family, Benjamin dedicated his life to a military career. However, his service to the army was not that of a soldier, but rather in the field of medicine.

In 1833, at the age of 32, Benjamin married Agnes Isabel Rooke, his first cousin and ten years his junior. By this time, he had already earned several medical degrees. The couple left England and moved to India where Benjamin continued to pursue his medical career, eventually achieving the role of Director General of the Medical Department in Bombay.

He served in the army during the 1839 storming of the Fortress of Ghuznee, Afghanistan, by British and Indian armies, being awarded the British campaign medal, the Ghuznee Medal.

Benjamin's career flourished in India and his contributions in the medical field were recognized by his receiving the prestigious appointment of Honorary Physician to Queen Victoria. The appointment of a physician to the Honorary Medical Staff of the Sovereign was first granted to the Indian Medical Service by a Royal Warrant of the Queen issued February 1, 1859, para. 15, which stated:

Six of the most meritorious medical officers of the Army shall be named My Honorary Physicians, and six, My Honorary Surgeons.

Benjamin was one of the originating six officers to receive this appointment and was noted in *A History of the Indian Medical Service, 1600-1913*, Vol. II:

The first officers to receive these appointments were gazetted from 6th September, 1861. Their names were - -

Honorary Physicians to the Queen - -

. . .

Principal I.G. Benjamin Proctor Rooke, Bombay.

While residing in India, three children were born to Benjamin and his wife Agnes: Agnes Emma (b.1835); Clement George Turner (Aubrey's father) (b.1837); and, Cresswell Keane Charles (b.1839). After only 24 years of marriage Agnes died in Bombay on July 15, 1847, at the age of 46.

By 1866, Benjamin had returned to England and, at the age of 65, started another family with his new spouse, Hannah Simpson. He went on to have four more children with his second wife: Benjamin Proctor Simpson (b.1866); Ernest Gilbert (b.1873); Charles Proctor (b.1876 – the same year his grandson, Aubrey, was born); and, Beatrice Mary (b.1877). At the time of the birth of his last child, Benjamin was 76 years old! He died ten years later in 1887 in Reigate, Surrey, England.

THOMAS CHARLES BYDE ROOKE

(1806-1858) – (Great-Uncle)

THOMAS CHARLES BYDE ROOKE

T.C.B. Rooke (Photo Credit: Wikimedia Commons;
TCBRookes.jpg; Hugo Stangenwald)

EDUCATION AND EARLY YEARS

T.C.B. ROOKE WAS BORN in 1806 in Hertford, England, the second son of Thomas Wildman Rooke and his wife Sarah Paillet Draper. He received his education at Christ's College Hospital in Hertford and graduated from the Royal College of Surgeons in London in 1826. Once his education was complete, it was pre-determined that T.C.B. would follow the family tradition of serving in the Royal Navy. However, his career path and his life did not play out as expected.

We know Aubrey Rooke left his British homeland due to poor health. However, the reason his great-uncle, T.C.B. Rooke, emigrated from England is not as clear. It seems there are two theories surrounding his departure.

In an article of the Hawaiian newspaper *The Polynesian* dated December 11, 1858, it stated the following:

Having in course of time removed to London to study his profession, and at an early age received his diploma, he felt desirous of seeing foreign parts, and with that view, as surgeon, joined a whaleship bound for the then romantic South-Sea fisheries.

A different scenario, however, is suggested in several other sources, including by a local Hawaiian reporter in her "Tales About Hawaii" column in the *Honolulu Star-Bulletin* dated December 16, 1955, referenced in the Hawaii Medical Journal as follows:

Dr. Rooke fell in love with a woman beneath his station, and, quarrelling with his father, gave up his career in the Navy and became a surgeon on a whaling ship bound for the South Seas.

This scenario was also confirmed by T.C.B.'s nephew, Cresswell Paillet Rooke, in a letter written to the Hawaiian Historical Society in 1930:

The story goes that the Hawaiian Rooke quarrelled with his father over a marriage he wished to make in England and left England for good never to return...

Whether the reason was for adventure or the love of a woman he could not have, T.C.B. Rooke left England, landing in Lahaina in 1829, and then on to Honolulu, where he remained until his death 30 years later. You can decide which scenario to believe.

Unlike his great-nephew, Aubrey Rooke, who chose to give up an inheritance rather than his British citizenship, Dr. Rooke had no difficulty with this and became a naturalized citizen of the United States on July 9, 1844.

MARRIAGE

After sailing aboard a whaling ship, T.C.B. arrived in Honolulu and, in 1830, married into the Royal Family of the Kingdom of Hawaii. His wife, Grace Kamaikui Young, was a Hawaiian high chiefess and the second daughter of the Englishman John Young, chief military advisor, friend, and counsellor of King Kamehameha I. It is said the two were a good match because Dr. Rooke was "a man of rare cultivation and refinement, with an outgoing and cheery disposition that complemented Grace's natural bashfulness."

Dr. Rooke and his wife, Grace, had no children of their own. However, in 1836, they adopted the infant daughter of Grace's sister in adherence to an ancient Hawaiian custom. This baby girl would grow up to become the very popular and much loved queen of Hawaii, Queen Emma, through her marriage to King Kamehameha IV.

MEDICAL CAREER

Dr. Rooke was a very important and influential man in his new homeland. His distinguished career led him to hold numerous high-level positions during his lifetime, including:

- Physician to the Royal Court;
- Friend and adviser to the Royal Family;
- Port Physician;

- One of the ten signers of the charter of incorporation of the Hawaiian Medical Society;
- Appointed to the first Board of Health and served as Chairman;
- Elected surgeon to a volunteer company known as the Hawaiian Guards;
- Under an Order of King Kamehameha III in 1850, a Board of Health was created and Dr. Rooke was appointed to it and served as Chairman. On the 50th anniversary of the formation of the Board of Health the Honolulu newspaper, *The Pacific Commercial Advertiser*, dated December 12, 1900, detailed the Order that had been proclaimed by the king those 50 years earlier as follows:

Be it known to all whom it may concern that we, by and with the advice of our Privy Council, hereby empower and authorize Dr. T.C.B. Rooke, Dr. George A. Lathrop, Benjamin F. Hardy, G.W. Hunter, C. Hoffman, M.D., Richard Hill Smythe and W. Newcomb to act as a Board of Health (four of them to be a quorum) for the good of the inhabitants of Honolulu, and we hereby authorize them to communicate, respecting the same, with the Governor of our Island of Oahu, and to point out to him everything that in their opinion ought to be done or undone, removed or procured, for the preservation (from?) (sic) and cure of contagious, epidemic and other diseases, and more especially of cholera, as may have occurred to each of them on the day preceding.

Our Minister of the Interior is charged with the execution of this our order.

Done in our Privy Council this 13th day of December, 1850.

KAMEHAMEHA

POLITICAL ACHIEVEMENTS

In addition to his medical interests, Dr. T.C.B. Rooke had political aspirations as well. He represented the constituents of the Honolulu district for two terms as a member of the House of Representatives (1851-1855). During the reign of King Kamehameha III, he held the office of Chamberlain to the Royal Household, and served on the Privy Council.

COMMUNITY SERVICE

Dr. T.C.B. Rooke was very involved in community service and participated in various clubs and societies. He brought along with him from his British homeland the societies of the Free Masons and Odd Fellows Clubs, to which he attained the highest levels. He was also one of the first members of the Mechanic's Benevolent Union, and sat as a member of the Board of Trustees of the Oahu Charity School.

INTERESTS

In addition to Dr. Rooke's professional, political, and community interests, he was one of the pioneers of the cultivation of coffee, becoming a charter member of the Royal Hawaiian Agricultural Society. Meteorology also fascinated him, and he was known to keep tables of his observations. As well, philanthropy was very important to Dr. Rooke, as was caring for the less fortunate.

LAND OWNER

In 1830, Dr. Rooke built a two-storey "mansion" known as "Rooke House". It was located on the southwest corner of Beretania and Nu'uanu Avenue, bordered by Fort Street and Chaplain Lane. Decorated in the British style, it was one of the largest private homes in Honolulu at the time, being used for many purposes including Dr. Rooke's medical clinic and dispensary, a library, and to hold elaborate parties and receptions. Unfortunately, the house has not survived and the land is now a parking lot.

In addition to his primary residence, over the years Dr. Rooke purchased many parcels of land which, upon his death, formed the bulk of his estate and would become the centre of contentious litigation. A few of the properties included a part of Nu'uanu Valley called Waolani (also known as "Rooke's Valley"). There was also property owned on the island of Kaua'i, as well as land where the current Oahu Country Club golf course is located.

DEATH

Dr. Rooke landed in the Hawaiian Islands in 1829 as a young man of 23, living there until his death on November 28, 1858, at the age of 52. While he passed away at a young age and many years were still ahead of him, his accomplishments were many and his legacy lives on today with the Queen's Hospital, created and built by his daughter, Queen Emma, who was greatly influenced by her father.

The announcement of his death was reported in *The Polynesian* on December 11, 1858, as follows:

Our late townsman T.C.B. Rooke Esq., died of apoplexy, at Kailua, Hawaii, on Sunday the 28th Nov. ult., at 1 o'clock P.M. He was attacked in the first instance at about 6 o'clock in the morning of the same day, when a messenger was instantly despatched for Dr. Herrick of South Kona, who arrived without loss of time and perceived at once that the patient was beyond recovery, and approved entirely of what had been done previous to his coming. The same day his Majesty caused measures to be taken to secure the services of two vessels to convey the Royal party and the remains of the deceased to Honolulu, but owing to a blow from the Southward, and other detentions, the embarkation was deferred till Saturday afternoon last, and their Majesties did not land till Tuesday morning. Soon after daylight of that day, however, news of the melancholy event became current in Honolulu, and produced a very general gloom among all classes, native and foreign, and when the "Mary" came in sight, the various flags in the harbor and on shore, that had been hoisted to welcome back the Royal family, were lowered to the half-mast.

Dr. T.C.B. Rooke was held in the highest esteem and regard by the citizens of his adopted country, and earned their respect as a generous and benevolent man. That same newspaper article went on to describe Dr. Rooke's caring and philanthropic nature:

… deeply impressed with the want of hospitals for sick natives, every morning [he] threw open the doors of his dispensary to many who could not otherwise have procured advice or medicines. Besides the amount of physical relief which he thus achieved it must have been a balm to the minds of many suffering wretches to know that what they claimed in vain as members of a community was accorded to them upon the broader though simper basis of a common humanity.

The article continued and reported that members of the medical community honoured Dr. Rooke at a meeting of the Hawaiian Medical Society with the following resolutions:

Whereas, it has pleased Divine Providence to remove from our midst, our brother T.C.B. Rooke, therefore, be it Resolved,

1st. That we have learned with deep sorrow and regret the sad news of the sudden and unexpected death of our colleague Dr. T.C.B. Rooke.

2d. That, in him, we have lost not only the Senior member of our Profession here, whose labors among this people and community during

*his long residence on these Islands, have secured for him an endur-
ing place in the memory of the Hawaiian nation; but, also, a brother
whose strict sense of professional propriety in his relations to us, as well
as to those entrusted to his care, have won for him our lasting esteem
and respect.*

*3d. That we offer our warmest sympathy to the afflicted widow and
family of the deceased…*

It is hard to believe that Aubrey Rooke, clerk for the Hudson Bay
Company in a small town in the Saskatchewan prairies, had a great-uncle
who lived and worked with the Royal Family of Hawaii, raised a girl who
would one day become queen, and contributed to such a degree in his
new homeland that he received the distinct honour of being laid to rest in
the Royal Mausoleum of Hawaii (known as Mauna `Ala) together with
members of the Royal Family of the Hawaiian Islands.

Royal Mausoleum, Honolulu (Photo Credit: Flickr – Wally Gobetz)

QUEEN EMMA OF HAWAII

(1836-1885) – (Cousin)

QUEEN EMMA OF HAWAII

COUSIN TO A QUEEN

HOW MANY OF US can say we are related to royalty? Aubrey Rooke could. Rooke's great-uncle, Dr. T.C.B. Rooke, and his wife Grace, could not have children so were promised a baby from Grace's sister in accordance with an ancient Hawaiian tradition called *hānai*. Upon the birth in 1836, the baby was handed over to the Rookes with the words spoken by the natural parents, "Nau ke keiki kukae a na'au" ("I give you this child intestines and all"). She was wrapped in a cloth, given the name Emma, and at that moment became Aubrey Rooke's cousin.

T.C.B. Rooke, Emma, Grace Kamaikui Young (Photo Credit: Wikimedia Commons; Rookes in 1853.jpg; Hugo Stangenwald)

The young Emma lived a life of wealth and privilege. The family was prominent in society, with her adoptive mother being a Hawaiian high chiefess and her adoptive father a highly regarded physician in the community who also worked for and socialized with the Hawaiian royal family. Dr. T.C.B. Rooke was deeply devoted to his adopted daughter and wanted her to have the cultural advantage of both her Hawaiian and British parents. Her formal education began with her enrollment in the Royal School for the Chief's Children. However, once that school closed, arrangements were made for Emma to be homeschooled. Her father ensured that a proper British education was provided, including tutors and books being sent from England. The books received were of such a large extent that they became the best library in Honolulu.

Queen Emma (Photo Credit: Wikimedia Commons; Queen Emma of Hawaii, retouched photo by J.J. Williams.jpg)

Due to her father's great influence on her, Emma grew up to be a very accomplished young woman and, on June 19, 1856, at the age of 20, Emma married King Kamehameha IV. Aubrey Rooke's cousin had become queen of the Hawaiian Islands.

THE QUEEN'S HOSPITAL

In the 1850s, the need for hospitals for the Hawaiian citizens was extreme. According to Richard A. Greer in his article, "The Founding of the Queen's Hospital":

Year by year disease and death exerted relentless pressure on the island's population. Failing in numbers and vigor, the Hawaiian nation seemed to be plunging toward extinction.

By January of 1854 the islands were just fighting free of a smallpox epidemic that had taken perhaps as many as 6,000 lives. The epidemic had given proof of the miserable lack of facilities to care for the stricken. Makeshift pesthouses were swamped with cases. But even under normal conditions there was no such thing as hospital care for the average Hawaiian. Since 1833 there had been hospitals, some better and some worse, for various nationalities of foreign seamen; in addition, a few doctors had now and then set up private hospitals for paying patients. Nearly all of these were foreigners, too.

With the smallpox epidemic of 1853, the improvement of health conditions for the local Hawaiian people had begun with King Kamehameha III. Upon his death in December, 1854, Prince Alexander Liholiho came to the throne in January, 1855, taking on the title King Kamehameha IV. The 21-year-old monarch's first priority was the health and well-being of his people, recognizing the importance and need of a hospital. Due to the influence and upraising Emma received from her father, she joined her husband in his strong desire to construct hospitals on the islands that would facilitate the treatment of the local Hawaiian people. As such, one of the main focuses during her reign as queen was the creation of a hospital.

The king began work immediately, passing legislation to establish hospitals on the islands to "treat sick and needy Hawaiians". As the government was in financial difficulty, the king and his queen personally undertook the mission to gain support for the hospital and raise the required funds to finance its construction. From their position of power and wealth, they were able to fund such a venture and the Queen's Medical Centre was established. Unfortunately, Dr. Rooke, who inspired Emma to create such a facility, did not live to see the project completed. However, to pay tribute to the contributions he made to the medical community, some of his medical instruments were donated to the Hospital.

The Queen's Hospital remains open to this day in downtown Honolulu and is the largest private non-profit hospital in Hawaii – a fitting tribute to the generous and compassionate Queen Emma – characteristics instilled in her by her father, Dr. T.C.B. Rooke.

Although worlds away, and several decades apart, you could find both Queen Emma and Aubrey Rooke walking the hallways of their respective hospitals visiting the patients. That same spirit of compassion and kindness that Dr. Rooke imparted in his daughter would also be demonstrated years later by his great-nephew, Aubrey.

CONTRIBUTIONS TO YOUTH

Aubrey Rooke was deeply involved with the youth in Fort Qu'Appelle, and worked to inspire and encourage them by organizing various sports teams. Queen Emma, also worked to achieve those same goals in Hawaii, establishing several schools including St. Cross School in Maui, and St. Andrew's Priory School for Girls in Honolulu. She was particularly interested in educating the girls and providing them with the same educational opportunities that the boys received. She specifically sought out these girls, encouraging them to attend school and providing personal scholarships.

CHURCH CONSTRUCTION

Under the influence and guidance of her British father, Dr. Rooke, Emma was raised in the Anglican faith. She and her husband, King Kamehameha IV, were responsible for bringing the Anglican faith to the Hawaiian Islands and were instrumental in the fundraising and construction of St. Andrew's Cathedral in Honolulu.

GENEROSITY

As was true with her cousin, Aubrey, it was said that Queen Emma *"disbursed much of her means in a quiet way, among the poor and the sick. She gave freely to people who were in need." "Hers was that charity which does not consider self."*

JOY AND SORROW

While T.C.B. Rooke had set up his daughter for a life of wealth, privilege, and happiness, she also experienced great loss and sadness. On May 20, 1858, Queen Emma gave birth to a son, Prince Albert Edward. Upon the prince's birth, the Queen of England, Queen Victoria, was asked to be the godmother to the child and the request was granted. Unfortunately, before the prince could be baptized, he became seriously ill and died at the age of four due to a "brain fever", now known as meningitis.

To add to Emma's grief, on November 28, 1863, just 15 months after the passing of her young son, her husband King Kamehameha IV died. The cause of his death was due to recurring chronic asthma, although some say it was from a broken heart from the loss of his son. The king was 29 years old. Emma became a widow at the age of 27.

ROYAL PEN PALS

With the social skills and education provided by her father that would lead her to one day become queen of the Hawaiian Islands, and in her role as queen, Emma formed a strong personal connection with Queen Victoria.

Through decades of correspondence, an enduring friendship arose between the two monarchs. Despite the numerous differences between Queen Emma and Queen Victoria, their mutual love of England, devotion to family, and their shared grief with the loss of sons and husbands bound them together.

From 1862-1882 letters went back and forth across the ocean. It began in September, 1862, with Queen Emma's thanking Queen Victoria for consenting to be her child's godmother and to announce of the death of that child, a portion of which reads:

Palace of Honolulu   *10th September 1862*

As a wife and fond mother, my heart overflows with gratitude to your Majesty, for the honour which you have been so graciously pleased to render to the King, my husband, and to our only son, in condescending to become his sponsor, at his baptism.

It was the cherished ambition of the King and myself, ever since the birth of our child, to obtain for him the enviable honour conferred on him by Your Majesty, and that he should bear the name of Albert.

Bu, alas! Your Majesty's spiritual relation to my beloved child has been of short duration, for it pleased Almighty God, in his inscrutable Providence, to call him away from this world, on the 17th August, only a few days after his baptism.

While our hearts are melted by this deep bereavement, his father and I find comfort in the thought that the departed has gone to Heaven, to mingle with the blessed; while as your Godson, and under a name dear to Your Majesty, his memory will ever be cherished by us and by our People.

The splendid gift which Your Majesty has been pleased to send in token of regard to the late Prince of Hawaii, will be preserved as a precious relic, to be venerated by the latest member of our Dynasty.

With that depth of feeling which is fully known to the heart of none but a mother, I pray Your Majesty to accept my thanks for Your Royal benevolence towards me and mine; and may God grant you his Grace, through life, and at the last a Crown of Immortal Glory.

Your Good & Grateful friend

Emma

The gift of which Queen Emma discusses is a sterling silver christening cup which is on exhibit at the Queen's Summer Palace in Honolulu.

Queen Victoria responded with great compassion and friendship:

Windsor Castle   February 14, 1863
Madam,

I thank you for your kind letter, and for the expressions of gratitude which it contains for my having accepted the Office of Godmother to the young Prince, your son.

As a Mother you will understand how fully I am able to appreciate the depth of your grief, at the sad loss which so soon succeeded to the Holy Ceremony.

As a wife I can sincerely hope that you may be spared the heavier blow which has plunged me into life long sorrow, - but which makes my heart tenderly alive to all the sorrows of others.

May that God, to whose promises we can alone look for consolation, soften the blow that has fallen upon you, and give you comfort in the knowledge of your beloved Child's present happiness and in the blessed prospect of an everlasting reunion with him hereafter.

I remain
Your Majesty's
Sincere friend
Victoria R.

Up until this point, the two women had never met in person. However, such was their friendship that in 1865 Emma would have occasion to travel to England to visit the British monarch. Upon her arrival in England, she was given the rare honour of spending a night in Windsor Castle with the British Royal Family. After one of their meetings, Queen Victoria wrote of Queen Emma:

After luncheon I received Queen Emma, the widowed Queen of the Sandwich Islands of Hawaii. Met her in the Corridor & nothing could be nicer or more dignified than her manner. She is dark, but not more so than an Indian, with fine features & splendid soft eyes. She was dressed in just the same widow's weeds as I wear. I took her into the White Drawingroom, where I asked her to sit down next to me on the sofa. She was much moved when I spoke of her great misfortune in losing her husband and only child. She was very discreet and would only remain a few minutes...

These personal meetings, together with the years of correspondence, served to create a bond that existed until Queen Emma's death.

DEATH OF A MONARCH

Beginning in 1883, Emma began experiencing several small strokes. She died in 1885 at the age of 49, thus ending the life of one of the most influential figures in Hawaiian history.

The lives of Queen Emma and her father, Dr. T.C.B. Rooke, were ones of affluence and prestige – a striking contrast to Aubrey Rooke's life of obscurity and near poverty in the hills of Fort Qu'Appelle, Saskatchewan. However, the same characteristics of duty, selfless generosity, and community service in support of education, health, and the well-being of others were demonstrated through the generations: from great-uncle, to royal cousin, and many years later to Aubrey Rooke.

CRESSWELL KEANE CHARLES ROOKE
(1839-1903) – (Uncle)

CRESSWELL KEANE
CHARLES ROOKE

AUBREY ROOKE'S UNCLE, CRESSWELL Keane Charles Rooke, became an important figure in the Rooke family legacy – first as a dedicated and devoted military man, and also the individual who successfully returned the Hawaiian lands purchased by T.C.B. Rooke back into the family's possession.

Born in 1839 at Cannanore in the East Indies, Cresswell Keane Charles Rooke was the second son born to Benjamin and Agnes Rooke. The middle name "Keane" was chosen to honour his godfather, Lord Keane, whom his father was serving under at the time. He married Mary Payne in 1869, and they had three children: Mary Agnes (b.1870); Isabel Nina Emma (b.1871); and, Cresswell Paillet (b.1873).

C.K.C. Rooke's life was dedicated to the military, beginning with the purchase of a Captaincy. He carried the Colours of his Regiment of The Royal Scots (The Royal Regiment) in the first China War in 1860. Then, in 1868, he was appointed Adjutant of a Depot Battalion. Moving up the ranks to Colonel, Colonel Rooke served with the Royal Scots in

Africa and India, commanding the Second Battalion from 1887-1891. He retired from the military in 1896.

THE HAWAIIAN INHERITANCE – THE CASE OF THE BATTLING WILLS

During his lifetime, Dr. T.C.B. Rooke purchased numerous parcels of land on the Hawaiian Islands. Upon his death, a set of circumstances was triggered that would years later become the focus of prolonged and complex litigation, eventually ending up in the Supreme Court of Hawaii. In fact, the matter developed into the most controversial, high-profile court cases in Hawaiian history. Dr. Rooke's estate would also have an impact on the Rooke family for generations, ultimately resulting in an inheritance to his great-nephew, Aubrey Rooke.

The controversy began innocently enough when Dr. Rooke prepared his Last Will and Testament dated February 28, 1852. As was the usual custom, he left his estate to his wife, Grace, and, upon his death on November 28, 1858, his estate flowed to her as per his wishes.

Grace passed away eight years later on July 15, 1866. Upon Grace's death, the lands owned by Dr. Rooke were directed to his adopted daughter, Queen Emma, again in accordance with his Will.

From 1866 until her death in 1885, Queen Emma maintained the Rooke lands along with her own properties. In accordance with her Will, the two main beneficiaries of her estate were her cousin, Albert Kunuiakea, and the Queen's Hospital. When Kunuiakea died childless, the Hospital became the sole beneficiary.

The court case arose due to a conflict between Queen Emma's Will and Dr. Rooke's Will. The queen's Will directed her executor, Mr. Alexander J. Cartwright, to give the various parcels of Rooke lands which she had inherited from her father to the Queen's Hospital:

I give and devise to The Queen's Hospital aforesaid and its successors and assigns forever the following tracts, pieces or parcels of land, viz: 1st, The premises situate on Fort and Union Streets in said Honolulu known as the French Hotel premises and described in Royal Patent No. 635 to T.C.B. Rooke. 2nd, The premises corner of Beretania and Nuuanu streets; in said Honolulu, described in Royal Patent No. 83 to T.C.B. Rooke. 3rd, All those two pieces of land at Honuakaha, at the head of Queen street, in said Honolulu, and described in L.C. Award No. 677, and conveyed by W.C. Parke, as Marshal, to T.C.B. Rooke. 4th, Land of Hopenui, at Puunui, on the south side of Liliha, in said Honolulu, portion of Royal Patent No. 607 to T.C.B. Rooke. 5th, Land at Kaaihee, in said Puunui, being a portion of Royal Patent No. 607 to T.C.B. Rooke. 6th, Land of Luapalolo, in said Puunui, described in Royal Patent No. 606 to T.C.B. Rooke. 7th, The land situate at Niolopa, in said Nuuanu valley, and described in Royal Patent No. 606 to T.C.B. Rooke. 8th, Land of Waolani, in said Nuuanu valley, known as Rooke's valley, and described in Royal Patent No. 168 to T.C.B. Rooke. 9th.

However, according to Dr. Rooke's Will, he desired the disposition of his lands to be passed on to Emma with the following instructions upon her death:

… to be used and enjoyed by her during the term of her natural life, and her children forever, but should the aforesaid Emma Rooke decease before me, the said testator, or decease without leaving any issue then I hereby give and bequeath the same unto my nephew and godson, Cresswell Charles Keane Rooke, son of Benjamin Proctor and Agnes Rooke, formerly of Hertford, England, but now residing at Bombay, and his heirs forever.

While it was Queen Emma's wishes as set out in her Will that not only her own lands but also the Rooke lands would be left to the Queen's Hospital, someone across the ocean in England had other ideas.

The nephew of Dr. T.C.B. Rooke, Colonel Cresswell Charles Keane Rooke, living in Colchester, England, decided to dispute the Hospital's claim to the lands, and would set in motion the steps to claim what he believed was his rightful inheritance – a decision that would eventually impact Aubrey Rooke.

As it turned out, Col. Rooke was not the only interested party. In fact, there were three parties claiming a stake to the Rooke property:

- The Queen's Hospital – in accordance with Queen Emma's Will;
- The Bishop Estate – claiming one-fourth of the lands through Kamehameha IV, (Queen Emma's husband); and,
- Col. Cresswell Rooke – pursuant to the Will of his uncle, Dr. T.C.B. Rooke.

WEIGHING THE OPTIONS

Colonel Cresswell Rooke had to consider carefully whether to proceed with claiming his inheritance from Dr. T.C.B. Rooke's estate and weigh the pros and cons of such legal action. According to his son, Cresswell Paillet Rooke, some of the considerations and deliberations of the family were as follows:

It would cost a lot for the legal expenses and further it would be an unpopular win, did we win; and last but not least, my father hesitated on account of the opponent being a hospital. But he needed the money for himself and his family to go on living in the way he was accustomed to. My mother, on the other hand, said that the hospital had received a large sum on Queen Emma's death additional to what she had given them during her lifetime and further they had received for some years the income from T.C.B. Rooke's estate. She was undoubtedly right.

Finally it was decided to take the matter to the courts and my mother undertook to pay the expenses should the case go against us; on the other hand should we win, the property won would be equally divided between my father and mother (after expenses were paid). The hospital had received for some years the income from this estate (a pretty considerable sum) and this we decided we would not claim. Next, it was quite a toss-up as to what lawyer to engage and how to proceed and what chances of success were. The whole thing was a gamble, quite straight forward had it happened in England; but out there quite another matter.

[Letter dated Dec. 1962 from Cresswell Paillet Rooke to Ernest Greatorex]

COURT ACTION

The decision finally made, Col. Cresswell Rooke hired as his attorneys in Hawaii the Acting British Consul General, Mr. Thomas Rain Walker, and Mr. F.M. Swanzy. The claim was commenced in the lower courts of the Hawaiian Judiciary on October 4, 1897, and it soon became the talk of the town. It was of such importance to the community that it was reported in the Honolulu newspaper *The Hawaiian Star* on that very same day:

AN IMPORTANT CASE.

Will Involve Large Property Interests in Honolulu.

A most extraordinary case was filed in the Circuit Court today by C.K.C. Rooke, of England, against the Queen's Hospital Association… and trustees of the Bishop estate.

Mr. Rooke seeks to recover about 200 acres of valuable land in Honolulu known as the French Hotel premises, Queen Emma residence, land at Homuakaha, Niolopa, Puunui, Oliku and Waoloni.

The Hawaiian Star continued its reporting the next day, October 5, 1897, with the headlines:

Half A Million Involved
Was Queen Emma Heir to Her Son?
If the Courts Decide in the Negative the Queen's
Hospital Association Loses Its Legacy

The article continued:

An exceedingly interesting point has been raised for the courts of Hawaii to determine in the important suit brought in the Circuit Court by Colonel Cresswell Keane Charles Rooke against the Queen's Hospital Association and the trustees of the Bernice Pauahi Bishop estate.

It is whether Queen Emma owned the property in fee simple left by Dr. Thomas Charles Byde Rooke, her adopted father, or whether she simply held a life interest in the property.

. . .

Colonel Rooke, who is a retired English army officer, having seen many years of active service in India, as well as the trustees of the B.P. Bishop estate, have shown a disposition to compromise the matter, but such an action would be embarrassing to the trustees of the Hospital Association, as their duty obliges them to hold on to the property entrusted to their care. Therefore, Colonel Rooke has taken the controversy to the courts to determine to whom the property really belongs. It cannot be said that the suit is an unfriendly one, as all three parties interested are anxious to have the cloud removed from the title of the land.

. . .

The property involved in the suit is given in the schedule appended to the petition as follows:

The French hotel premises, containing 86-100 of an acre,

Queen Emma residence, containing 1 5-100 acres,

Land at Honuakaha, Honolulu,

Land at Niolopa in Nuuanu valley, containing 8 89-100 acres,

Land at Puunui, containing 12 6-10 acres,

Land called Oliku, containing 25 and 9-10 acres,

Land in Nuuanu valley, known as Waolani, containing 61 1/2 acres.

A year later, in November, 1898, Circuit Court Judge Perry decided in favour of Col. Rooke. An article dated November 30, 1898, in *The Hawaiian Star* newspaper, featured the headlines:

Queen's Hospital Loses. Rooke Wins His Suit for the Premises. Judge Perry Declares Queen Emma's Bequest Was Not Legal – Appeal Will Be Taken.

The Judge's decision was that:

In my opinion it was the testator's intention to give to his adopted daughter Emma Rooke, after the death of his wife, a life estate, and that after her death, if she survived him and left issue surviving her, the property should go to her children absolutely, but that if she should die before the testator, or die without any issue surviving her, then the property should go to his nephew and godson, C.K.C. Rooke, the plaintiff herein.

In my opinion that intention is sufficiently expressed by the language of the will, and the title to the property passed to the plaintiff at Emma Rooke's death.

While Col. Cresswell Rooke had won his case, the battle was far from over. It was noted in the same newspaper article:

An appeal from this decision will be bitterly contested.

And, indeed, it was appealed. The matter proceeded to the Supreme Court of the Republic of Hawaii and, on May 11, 1900, Col. Rooke was successful once again. The final decision arrived at by Justice Frear was as follows:

> *Thus, in any view, whether Queen Emma took an estate tail, a fee simple conditional, a fee simple, a life-estate with vested remainder in the Prince or a life-estate with alternate contingent remainders in the Prince and Colonel Rooke, the latter, upon her death without leaving any issue surviving her, became entitled (by way of executory devise or remainder, as the case might be) to the lands in question in fee simple in possession.*
>
> [Rooke v. Queen's Hospital, 12 Haw. 375 (1900)]

After years of litigation, Col. Rooke's claim was successful and numerous properties handed down from his uncle, Dr. T.C.B. Rooke, were now in his possession.

REACTION TO COURT CASE

The landmark decision of the Supreme Court in favour of Col. Rooke sent shock waves throughout the island. The defeat in the court caused a considerable financial blow to the Queen's Hospital, as well as the loss of several scholarships and annuities to other beneficiaries derived from the rental income from the Rooke properties. As an additional financial consequence, back rents were owed to Col. Rooke, rents which had been received by the wrong party since 1885 – the year Queen Emma died.

The breaking news hit the Honolulu newspaper *The Hawaiian Star* dated May 11, 1900 (the day of the Supreme Court's landmark decision) with the headline:

Queen's Hospital Loses. Stripped of Property By The Supreme Court. All the Estate Upon Which it Depended for a Revenue Goes to Captain Rooke. Sweeping Decision.

The article continued:

The Supreme court this afternoon filed a decision in the case of C.K.C. Rooke vs. Queen's Hospital and Bishop estate, entirely in favor of the plaintiff. It is decided that Rooke is the rightful heir and possessor of all the property involved. The case has hung fire in the courts for several years.

The result of the decision is that the fine Queen's Hospital premises on Punchbowl street, Queen Emma Hall, facing Nuuanu avenue, and numerous other lots in town pass to Rooke.

What will be done with the hospital is a matter of most concern. As Rooke is in England, and never was in Honolulu, it is not supposed that he will take much interest in the hospital, and will want to get ever cent possible out of it. In this case the hospital will probably go unless some compromise can be effected.

With regard to the issue of back rents that were now owed to Col. Rooke by the Queen's Hospital, *The Hawaiian Star* commented on these financial complications in a May 14, 1900, article:

It is learned on excellent authority that Colonel Rooke will not make any claims for back rents. If he did it would be a very serious matter indeed for all concerned, as the benefits to the hospital have been accruing and used for many years.

In the Honolulu newspaper *The Pacific Commercial Advertiser* dated May 15, 1900, the court decision was reported as follows:

Rooke Decision Is Far Reaching. Queen's Hospital and Many Private Persons Lose Annuities by Court's Judgment.

The result of the lawsuit of Captain Rooke against the Queen's Hospital is far reaching in its effects, and many private annuities and revenues are summarily cut off by the recent decision. The Queen's Hospital loses a large share of its annual revenue. The decision is sweeping in character, and all other suits which have hinged on the one just ended, will be withdrawn from Court.

Also in an article of *The Pacific Commercial Advertiser* on May 17, 1900, the paper commented on Col. Rooke's gain and the hospital's loss:

The fifteen years' delay experienced by Dr. Rooke in coming into his property has probably benefitted him considerably, as the property is increasing in value, and will doubtless continue to do so for some time to come on account of the progressive period Honolulu has just entered into. The Queen's Hospital will lose proportionately by a similar process of reasoning.

Nine months after the court decision, the newspapers were still commenting on it. Again in the Honolulu newspaper *The Pacific Commercial Advertiser* on February 12, 1901:

The decision which gave such a vast amount of property to Colonel Rooke was a sweeping one.

THE AUCTION – MARCH, 1901

After years of litigation, the battle was over and the victory went to Col. Cresswell Rooke. As a result, a man living across the ocean in Colchester, England, was now in possession of numerous pieces of valuable Hawaiian properties – some located in the business district of Honolulu, as well as various parcels of land located in the countryside just south of what is now the Oahu Country Club. His next decision would be: What would he do with these lands? He decided to put up for auction the downtown properties.

The auction was highly anticipated in the community as noted in the edition of the Honolulu newspaper, *The Pacific Commercial Advertiser*, dated February 12, 1901, a whole month prior to the auction date:

Colonel C.K.C. Rooke, the British officer who, last May, became possessed of some of the most valuable real estate in Honolulu by the decision of the Hawaiian Supreme Court, is to sell all his holdings at public auction next month. The property offered is gilt-edged inside business realty, located in the heart of the busiest section of the city, and the bidding is certain to be the liveliest Honolulu has ever seen.

It was March 16, 1901, and the big day had finally arrived! Some of the most valuable property in downtown Honolulu was going to be sold! *The Evening Bulletin* reported the attendance of all the high rollers from the community with a whopping $20 million dollars' worth of investment funds burning a hole in their collective pockets. The scene was set as follows:

Valuable Property Was Sold Today.

The event of the day in real estate circles was the sale of valuable property belonging to the C.K.C. Rooke estate at the auction rooms of Jas. F. Morgan. When the 12 o'clock whistles blew, there was a great crowd in the rooms. From estimates made by one who is well acquainted with the financial standing of the various interests of the city, there was in the neighborhood of $20,000,000.00 of capital represented.

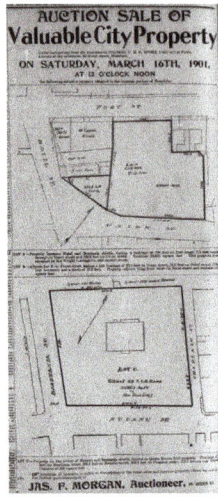

(Photo Credit: Wikimedia
Commons; Auction Sale
of Valuable City Property,
Advertiser, February 14,
1901.jpg; The Pacific
Commercial Advertiser)

As described in *The Independent*:

At noon today Jas. F. Morgan's auction rooms were the centre of attraction on account of the sale of valuable city property by order of the attorneys of Col. C.K.C. Rooke, of London, England. The place was packed with people of all standing in the community.

Three properties were on the auction block. The first one up was Lot B of the Rooke property located at the intersection of Union and Hotel streets, with an area of 3,284 sq. ft., and a starting bid of $15,000.00. After outbidding Judge Humphreys, Mr. Harry Armitage was the proud new owner, with a final bid of $22,400.00.

Lot A was next under the hammer, being 28,621 sq. ft. of property between Hotel and Beretania streets. The start bid was $85,000.00, however one of the wealthy attendees was looking to undercut the price and attempted to begin the bidding at only $50,000.00. The ever-so-wise auctioneer smiled and advised he already had a bid of $75,000.00. After some back and forth between the participants, it was finally sold to Mr. Wolters for $80,500.00.

The final piece of land up for auction that day was located at the corner of Nuuanu and Beretania streets, known as "Queen Emma Hall" (formerly the Queen's residence). With a starting bid of $95,000.00, a sale was never achieved and the property was withdrawn. It appeared the gentlemen in attendance were looking for a bargain that day and the price was just too rich for their blood.

The proceeds from the sale of the two Rooke properties totalled $102,900.00 in 1901. Given the value of the U.S. dollar in 2021, that amount would be the equivalent of $3,233,118.00, not even taking into account the increase in the real estate market in Hawaii since 1901.

THE QUEEN'S BRACELETS – DEAL STRUCK WITH HOSPITAL

In April, 1903, just prior to the death of Col. Cresswell Rooke a few months later in August of that year, his son, Mr. Cresswell Paillet Rooke, travelled to Hawaii to finalize some of his father's remaining affairs.

In exchange for Col. Rooke's generosity in waiving the back rents owed to him by the Queen's Hospital, his son, Cresswell Paillet Rooke, requested two bracelets belonging to Queen Emma be given as family heirlooms. He had seen the queen wear them in a photograph and wrote about the request as follows:

> I wrote to the Queen's Hospital and they replied that they knew where the bracelets were, but they (as bracelets) had no use for them. I replied that, in that case, surely they were of more importance to Colonel Rooke (my father) than to anyone else; and I suggested that the Hospital Trustees should present them to my father; after all they had received much from Queen Emma, and a goodly sum from my father. And so it came about.

[Letter dated Dec. 1962 from Cresswell Paillet Rooke to Ernest Greatorex]

The obtaining of these bracelets was reported in the Honolulu newspaper *The Pacific Commercial Advertiser* dated March 26, 1904, with the headline reading:

Victoria's Gift To Queen Emma To Leave Hawaii.

Jewelled Bracelet Containing Medallion Portrait and Lock of Hair of England's Sovereign Will Repose in Possession of Creswell Rooke.

The article continued:

Two of the prized heirlooms of the Queen Emma collection, which are closely related in island history to Queen Victoria and the Duke of Edinburgh, will leave Hawaii on the next steamer and be returned to England whence they came thirty-five and forty years ago respectively.

The bracelets were described in detail as follows:

One is the bracelet presented by Queen Victoria to Emma in 1865. It is of fine English gold, very heavy and broad, with the inscription inside: "Victoria R-27 November, 1865." The top stone is a large onyx covering a locket in which is a medallion miniature of Victoria. The flat portion below the onyx stone encloses in glass a lock of Victoria's hair, which is a dark golden brown color. The medallion shows Victoria in widow's weeds, a picture well known. She sits in a pensive attitude at a table leaning her chin up on one hand.

The second bracelet, the present of the Duke of Edinburgh, is also of gold. The bracelet, which is very broad, is set with a beautiful amethyst surmounted by a sunburst of diamonds and pearls. The large stone is also surrounded by pearls.

The bracelets remained in the possession of the Rooke family in England until 1958, when the Queen Victoria bracelet was returned once again to Hawaii to be displayed at Queen Emma's Summer Palace. Also returned to Hawaii at this time by the Rooke family was:

> ... one of Queen Victoria's many letters to Queen Emma, framed and apparently this disappeared 'en route'; I remember Queen Victoria's letter ended 'With renewed expressions of friendship and esteem.' I remain, Your Majestys Appreciated friend Victoria R.

[Letter dated Dec. 1962 from Cresswell Paillet Rooke to Ernest Greatorex]

The generous move by Cresswell Paillet Rooke to accept the bracelets in exchange for forgiving of the debt of back rents owed by the hospital saved it considerable financial difficulties.

NAPOLEON'S HAIR

At one time, the Rooke family had been in possession of another item of special historic significance – a locket containing a lock of Napoleon Bonaparte's hair. It was specifically mentioned in Col. Rooke's Last Will and Testament as follows:

> To my son Cresswell Paillet one hundred pounds also my gold locket containing the hair of the Emperor Napoleon to be retained as an heirloom.

How does someone come into possession of such an object? It seems that a Mrs. Emma Rooke (wife of Col. Benjamin Rooke) would occasionally visit Aubrey's family at their home in Colchester, England. During the Peninsular War (1807-1814), Col. Benjamin Rooke served under his uncle, Col. Robert Dudgeon, of the 66th Regiment. This Regiment had two battalions stationed on St. Helena to guard Napoleon during his exile from Italy.

Cresswell Paillet Rooke, described how the lock of hair was obtained:

> Dudgeon was a Major then and was what was called 'Captain of The Guard' and on Napoleon's death he cut off a piece of Napoleon's hair

and later had it fixed into a locket and backed with Mother of Pearl, and inscribed 'Napoleons hair cut from Napoleons had by Colonel Dudgeon 66th Regiment'.

[Letter dated Dec. 1962 from Cresswell Paillet Rooke to Ernest Greatorex]

While Cresswell Paillet Rooke does not explain exactly how his branch of the family came into possession of the locket of hair, one could reasonably assume that Col. Dudgeon left it to his nephew, Col. Benjamin Rooke, as they had served together during the war. Then, at some point, Benjamin's wife Emma gifted it to Aubrey's family during one of her visits.

FINALIZING THE ESTATE – RUBBING ELBOWS WITH THE RICH AND FAMOUS

After years of litigation in the Hawaiian courts, Col. Cresswell Rooke finally received his well-fought-for inheritance. Unfortunately, his good fortune would be short-lived. On August 17, 1903, three years after the Hawaiian Supreme Court had rendered its final decision in his favour, the Colonel passed away in his home in Colchester, England. Just five months prior to his death, on March 30, 1903, he had appointed his son, Cresswell Paillet Rooke, to be his Power of Attorney in resolving and finalizing all outstanding Hawaiian matters. At the time, he was still in possession of ten pieces of property previously owned by his uncle, Dr. T.C.B. Rooke. Cresswell Paillet Rooke made the journey to the islands to wrap up his father's affairs.

While in Honolulu, Cresswell Paillet Rooke was received warmly by the high society of the island and was invited to many social functions. One prestigious event was a royal party reported in the Society column of *The Pacific Commercial Advertiser* on April 26, 1903, as follows:

Prince and Princess Kalanianaole gave an elaborate poi supper on Tuesday evening at Pualeilani, Waikiki, in honor of Miss Nalani Jones, as a farewell function preparatory to her departure in the Alameda the following day for Mare Island, where she will be the guest of Commander and Mrs. Dixon for four or five months. The table was daintily decorated in pink and green. In the center were jardinieres filled with pink asters and pink roses profusely intermingled. At each guest's place was a lei favor of pink carnation and maile. The place cards were pink, with the Prince's coat of arms and motto, "Kulia i ka Nuu," emblazoned thereon in gold and green. Following the supper dancing was enjoyed in the old lanai. Among the guests were Sir Somers Vine, Mr. Cresswell Rooke, Governor Cleghorn, Captain Windham, R.N., and the ward-room officers of the British cruiser Amphitrite. Miss Jones received quite a floral send-off when the Alameda sailed.

Another fancy soiree was thrown by the attorney who had represented Col. Rooke in his successful lawsuit. The party was reported in the same newspaper on June 21, 1903:

Mr. and Mrs. Alfred Magoon entertained at a poi luncheon last Sunday at 1 p.m. The table decorations were in red and green. The center piece was a basket of maiden hair ferns caught at the handle by a knot of red satin ribbon. Sprays of maiden hair ferns and red carnations were strewn over the cloth. Among those present were Mr. and Mrs. Eben Low, Dr. and Mrs. Geo. Herbert, Mrs. Alice Hutchinson, Mr. Cresswell Rooke, Miss Mary Low, Mr. Gerrit Wilder, Miss Magoon, Mr. McGonigle.

PAYING THE PIPER

The controversial court case battling for Dr. T.C.B. Rooke's land meandered its way through the Hawaiian court system, eventually reaching its conclusion in the Supreme Court. During the final juncture of litigation, Col. Rooke had sought legal representation from attorney Mr. J. Alfred

Magoon, of the law firm Magoon & Silliman, who assumed carriage of the file.

While the eventual decision came down in May, 1900, it would be another eight years before all matters were resolved and Mr. Magoon received payment for his services. By this time, Col. Rooke had been dead for five years and his son, Cresswell Paillet Rooke, had assumed responsibility for resolving his father's estate. The case that had attracted such great attention in Hawaii was once again the focus of interest. An article in *The Hawaiian Star* dated October 9, 1908, reported:

Magoon's Fat Fee

According to a document filed this morning in the office of the Registrar of Conveyances Attorney J. Alfred Magoon of this city has come in for a pretty nice fee. The papers show where he has released all claims of whatever kind from the 'commencement of the world' till the present date against the Rooke estate, for the sum of $4,500.

Magoon represented the Rooke estate in this Territory in considerable litigation which he finally won through a decision of the Territorial Supreme Court. His fees were all arranged for on a contingent basis and now a final settlement has been made which gives Magoon the fee mentioned. It was received by him from Cresswell Pailett Rooke and the Venerable Archdeacon Edward Ambrose Hardy.

And with that, after over a decade of dispute and conflict regarding Dr. T.C.B. Rooke's estate had begun, the matter was finally concluded.

CRESSWELL PAILLET ROOKE
(1873-1966) – (Cousin)

CRESSWELL PAILLET ROOKE

Cambridge University class picture - Cresswell Paillet Rooke seated, 2nd row from bottom, 2nd from the right (Photo Credit: Cambridge University)

THE ROOKE FAMILY TREE can be traced back to Huguenot origins in the 17th century by way of the family name "Paillet". The name "Paillet" appears throughout the family tree, including Aubrey's first cousin, Cresswell Paillet Rooke, whose name was chosen to honour that lineage.

Born on June 28, 1873, at Aldershot, Hampshire, he was the third child of Col. Cresswell Keane Charles Rooke and his wife, Mary Payne.

Cresswell Paillet was quite a distinguished and impressive gentleman. His education began at Portsmouth Grammar, continued for a number of years with private tutors, and finally concluded with three terms at Cambridge University. Similar to Aubrey, languages came easy to Cresswell Paillet, being fluent in French, Latin and Greek.

Continuing the long-standing family tradition of military service, including that of his father, Cresswell Paillet became a soldier. He served as a Major with the Duke of Cambridge's Own (Middlesex) Regiment; Lieutenant-Colonel in the Royal Warwickshire Regiment; and, Lieutenant-Colonel with the Royal Air Force during World War I, receiving the Distinguished Service Order medal.

In 1915, he was wounded in battle in France and was sent home to England to recuperate. He was asked where he would like to be sent for his hospital stay and recalled the experience with an apparent sense of humour about the whole thing:

> *I mentioned London (as having well known hospitals); naturally I felt therefore that that was the last place I would be sent to!!! I was right for I found that I was finally deposited on a stretcher on a dusty platform, at Farnborough, Hampshire. As it happened I knew Farnborough well and was born at Aldershot nearby; but the interesting thing was that I found myself being taken to 'The Empress Eugenie's hospital' and duly deposited in through a window.*

[Letter dated Dec. 1962 from Cresswell Paillet Rooke to Ernest Greatorex]

During the war, wounded soldiers were accommodated on the grounds of Empress Eugenie's Estate at Farnborough in various chalets which normally would house visitors. There was also a chapel in which services were frequently held and which was the resting place of the late husband of the empress and the tomb of her son, the Prince Imperial.

Cresswell Paillet described a visit to his hospital bed one day by an interesting old lady:

I lay on my bed, wishing I were fit and back with the regiment, and I suddenly saw a little frail old lady pass my window, she entered, but I could not rise and she bade me remain as I was.

[Letter dated Dec. 1962 from Cresswell Paillet Rooke to Ernest Greatorex]

That "little frail old lady" was none other than the empress herself: Eugenie de Montijo (1826-1920); the 16th Countess of Teba; 15th Marchioness of Ardales; wife of Emperor Napoleon III; and, Empress of France from 1853 to 1870.

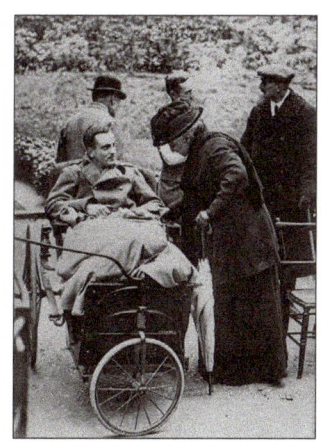

Empress Eugenie with an English soldier, 1914
(Photo Credit: Wikimedia Commons; Unknown Author)

The Empress Eugenie was Spanish born, but left for Paris due to the cholera outbreak. She was formally educated at a Parisian convent, and briefly attended a boarding school in England to learn English. Due to teasing, she attempted to run away to India, but was caught. Thereafter, she was educated at home, tutored by English governesses. She was very athletic, was rescued from drowning, and attempted suicide twice due to romantic "disappointments". Politics were of great interest to her and when her husband the emperor was away, she would act as regent. During the Franco-Prussian War in which the emperor participated, she managed the government in his absence. In her capacity as empress, she also travelled to Egypt to open the Suez Canal and often represented her husband in other affairs of state.

Portrait of Eugenie de Montijo (Photo Credit: Wikimedia Commons; Franz Xaver Winterhalter)

By the time Cresswell Paillet was recuperating from his war injuries on Empress Eugenie's Estate, the empress was a widow and her only son, the Prince Imperial, had been killed while fighting with the British in the

Zulu War. After leaving France, she took up residence at Farnborough, England, continuing to live with the same "pomp" as though she was still the empress.

Cresswell Paillet described his first encounter with the empress:

… that little shrunken old lady was still the Empress in manner and full of vitality. In her youth she had been one of the most beautiful ladies of Europe. She was full of fun and came daily to see me and I always spoke French, and she always spoke English and we laughed much at the rest.

[Letter dated Dec. 1962 from Cresswell Paillet Rooke to Ernest Greatorex]

The empress must have enjoyed his company as an invitation was extended for him to attend a lunch with some very prestigious guests:

The day before I was to be discharged and taken home to Colchester for daily visits to that Military Hospital, I was summoned to lunch with her at the Mansion. I hesitated, for my uniform tho now cleaned and patched, was I felt, hardly fit to 'accept' the 'Invitation'? I was reminded that her invitation was a Command!!! I literally collapsed inside with shame, but we both laughed.

Of course I enjoyed the lunch, a certain Prince Napoleon; the Duke of Alba there representing Spain in England; and two Belgian Princesses were there and I was put on the Empresses right. Everyone started speaking Spanish. Her Majesty apologized and pointed out that only English or French must be spoken; of course they all spoke English perfectly. When lunch was over, the Empress personally took me to see some of her treasures and 'enpassant'. I saw a picture of Gibraltar and to complete my blunders I said 'Your Majesty, a connection of mine Admiral Sir George Rooke captured Gibraltar, she froze; I quickly added 'he is dead now however' and we both laughed. I had forgotten she was Spanish.

The next day, my very dear mother motored over from Colchester to fetch me. The Empress said 'But we do not want him to go'.

[Letter dated Dec. 1962 from Cresswell Paillet Rooke to Ernest Greatorex]

The empress was a very grand and accomplished lady, and for Cresswell Paillet to have attracted her attention and been able to hold his own at a lunch with such distinguished guests speaks of his intelligence and manner.

Once settled at home, he requested a photograph of the empress:

I had a little snap shot of 'The Empress' and later I sent it to her Lady in Waiting; asking her to request the honour of Her Majestys signature to it. An answer informed me that there was refusal to my request. I felt deeply hurt for she had encouraged me to drop the ceremony at all times. A little later, I received a (picture) photo of Her Majesty as a very beautiful young woman, kneeling on her prie dieu and duly signed.

She evidently wished me to see her young, beautiful and yet on her knees.

[Letter dated Dec. 1962 from Cresswell Paillet Rooke to Ernest Greatorex]

Empress Eugenie, 1880 (Photo Credit: Wikimedia Commons; Empress Eugenie 1880.jpg; W. & D. Downey)

After his military service in the War, Cresswell Paillet continued to be involved in service to his country. He formed and commanded the No. 7 School of Military Aeronautics, Bath (1918-1919); was the Assistant Commandant of the Central Flying School (1919-1920); and the Commandant of the Royal Air Force Depot, Uxbridge (1920). He retired from service with the rank of Lieutenant-Colonel in 1926.

CLEMENT GEORGE TURNER ROOKE

(1837-1918) – (Father)

CLEMENT GEORGE TURNER ROOKE

MILITARY SERVICE WAS A way of life for another member of the Rooke family. Aubrey's father, Clement George Turner Rooke, was born in 1837 in Bombay, India, to Benjamin and Mary Rooke.

In 1855, at the age of 18, Clement joined the Bombay Native Infantry (a regiment government by the East India Company) as an Ensign. Two years later, at the age of 20, he had advanced to the role of Lieutenant in the 12th Regiment of the Bombay Native Infantry, later known as the 112th Infantry in the Indian Army. In 1862, the London Gazette announced his promotion to Captain of the 109th Regiment (Bombay Infantry) at 25 years of age.

When Clement was 34, he married Melissa Rebecca Powney, a woman who came from a prestigious family in her own right. Her father was Captain John Powney and her grandfather was Portlock Powney, a Member of Parliament for the British Government and Ranger of Home Park, Windsor. (This family lineage would make Aubrey the great-grand-son of an MP of the British Government.) Sadly, the couple were only married for six years before Melissa passed away, just two months after Aubrey's birth. Clement never re-married.

Clement's military career continued until approximately 1881, when he appears in the census at the age of 44, retired, a widow, and living with him a four-year-old Aubrey.

During his later years, Clement chose to live in a very unique way of life that was considered outside the realm of normal society at the time. He took up residence on a small fruit colony in Brookville, Stoke Ferry, Norfolk. The colony was considered a "bold experiment into alternative living" as it was based on a cooperative way of living – a gathering of people with a variety of skills and trades, making the group as self-sustainable as possible. The main pursuits were agricultural, such as fruit orchards, vegetable gardens, poultry farmers and egg producers. The colonists would sell their products to the local communities, as well as provide the necessary foods to their fellow residents. Over time, other tradespeople made the fruit colony home and contributed their particular skills to the group such as builders, carpenters, ironmongers, and a printer. By the time Clement shows up in Brookville in the 1911 census, its population had grown from 22 households to 33. The small colony had also added further services including a post office, shop, print works, jam factory, and a workshop that produced rustic furniture.

While the colony as an entity officially wound up in 1913, many of the residents remained and carried on with their activities and cooperative lifestyle.

Clement passed away in Brookville in 1918 at the age of 81.

ISABEL EMMA NINA ROOKE
(1871-1912) – (Cousin)

ISABEL EMMA NINA ROOKE

TRAGEDY STRIKES THE FAMILY

IN 1912, A DEVASTATING accident occurred that rocked the Rooke family and the British nautical community.

Isabel Rooke was born in Colchester, Essex, the second daughter of Cresswell Keane Charles Rooke. At the age of 38, Isabel married The Reverend John Craigie Leishman, a Chaplain in the British navy.

On March 15, 1912, Isabel Rooke, her husband, and their eight-month-old daughter, boarded the S.S. Oceana in London bound for Bombay. The Oceana was a 6,610 gross ton steamship with a length of 468.3 feet, two funnels, four masts, and could accommodate 250 people in 1st class and a further 160 passengers in 2nd class. Sailing on that day was a crew of 221, with only 41 passengers, the remainder of which were scheduled to board the ship when it docked at Marseilles.

The Oceana (Photo Credit: Wikimedia Commons; Oceana
(P. & O.) LCCN2014690211.tif; Bain News Service, Publisher)

In addition to being a passenger ship, the Oceana was also a cargo vessel, carrying on this trip a cache of £747,110 in gold and silver. Also on board, bound for Secunderabad, India, was a brass memorial plaque commemorating the 1st Nottingham regiments' sacrifice of 800 men (mostly to disease) during its service in the area from 1819-1838.

Unfortunately, the Leishmanns' journey was short-lived. One day into the trip, tragedy struck that would shake the Rooke family to the core. On March 16, 1912, at about 3:50 a.m., in the Strait of Dover just off Beachy Head, a German steel-hulled sail ship called the Pisagua hit the Oceana mid-ship, creating a 40 foot gash in her side. Passengers from the Oceana filed into the various lifeboats to escape the sinking ship. The Leishmanns were assigned to lifeboat No. 1 together with two seamen, Chantler and Carter, who, due to their naval experience, were put in charge. The family must have been so relieved to get into that lifeboat, but relief quickly turned to horror.

The Pisagua (Photo Credit: Wikimedia Commons; Jensen
Hamburger Viermaster Pisagua 1893.jpg; Alfred Jensen)

While the Oceana was still moving forward, the lifeboat was lowered down the side of the ship, hit the water at a 30 degree angle, and immediately became swamped and capsized. All the occupants in the lifeboat were thrown into the sea, except for a Miss Macfarlane who somehow managed to remain in the boat. Miraculously, both of the seamen made it back to the Oceana. However, in so doing, they left behind all those in the water, including Miss Macfarlane who remained in a semi-conscious state in the lifeboat. Once safe on board, the seamen failed to tell anyone about the woman they abandoned, who was eventually rescued by boats that had responded to the emergency. While she had escaped a horrible death, many were not so fortunate. Seven other passengers and ten crew were lost to the sea including Isabel, her husband, and their infant child. No effort was made by the crew to pick up the drowning people. Cowardice and incompetence were not borne solely by the crew alone, however. The Captain himself did not even inquire as to the status of those in the capsized boat until he was safely aboard one of the rescue ships.

The Oceana was towed to land, however she developed a severe list such that her propeller was above the waterline. The remaining crew on board transferred to the tow ship and the Oceana sank in less than 20 minutes. Her final resting place was close to the seaside resort community of Eastbourne and her masts and the tops of her funnels could be seen at low tide. A few months later, in July, 1912, the wreck was blown up by the Royal Navy as it posed a danger to shipping. Today it has become a popular diving site.

On April 30, 1912, a Formal Investigation commenced, with the owners of the Oceana claiming damages for the loss of the ship. Two months later, on June 25, 1912, presiding Judge Dickenson ruled:

> *The collision was caused by the wrongful act of the chief officer [of the Oceana] in attempting to cross ahead of [the Pisagua], and for this the court suspends his certificate of competency for six months.*
>
> *After the collision 17 lives were lost through the swamping of No. 1 life-boat. This was largely due to the error of judgment of the chief officer in lowering the boat while the vessel was still underway. For the failure to take adequate measures to rescue the persons thus thrown into the water the court severely censures the master and chief officer, and also attaches blame to the third officer.*

["Oceana" and "Pisagua", The Merchant Shipping Act, 1894, (No. 7539)]

At the end of the investigation, it was concluded that the Pisagua was not at fault due to a naval rule of the right-of-way: the "steam gives way to sail" rule.

One can only imagine the shock and deep sorrow experienced by the Rooke family when they learned of the devastating news of the loss of their loved ones. It was said in the community that after the accident "the life seemed to die in the [Rooke] house after that."

The collision of the Oceana and the loss of 17 lives also came as a huge shock to the British nautical community. In the aftermath of the event, it was determined that had the passengers simply remained on the Oceana rather than panic and rush to the supposed safety of the lifeboats, no loss of life would have occurred as the ship remained afloat for approximately six hours after the collision, providing plenty of time for assistance to arrive. However tragic this accident seemed at the time, it was foreshadowing something even more catastrophic – a month later almost to the day, on April 15, 1912, the Titanic hit an iceberg and sank.

Leishman family headstone – front
(Photo Credit: findagrave.com – Frank Grant)

Leishman family headstone – back
(Photo Credit: findagrave.com – Frank Grant)

CHARLES PROCTOR ROOKE

(1876-1913) – (Uncle)

CHARLES PROCTOR ROOKE

WILD WEST SHOOT OUT

ONLY 11 MONTHS AFTER the loss of three cherished lives of the Rooke family off the English coast, another devastating blow hit the family – this time in Canada.

While Aubrey's grandfather, Benjamin Proctor Rooke, resided in Bombay, India, and held the position of Honorary Physician to Queen Victoria and Director General of the Medical Department, his wife passed away making him a widower at the age of 56. He remained so until his marriage to Hannah Simpson at age 69, and had four more children with his second wife, one being Charles Proctor Rooke, born May 5, 1876, in Redhill, Surrey, England.

In 1895, at the age of 19, Charles Rooke made the trip from his homeland in England to Canada, the land of opportunity, as his nephew Aubrey had done three years earlier. Upon his arrival in Canada, Charles settled in the Holland, Manitoba area and like many immigrants to the country tried his hand at farming. However, as with the rest of the Rooke men, duty and service ran in his blood and he joined the North-West Mounted Police, serving with the force for five years, until 1905, when he was selected by the Manitoba Provincial Government to organize a group called the Manitoba Mounted Police. Their main focus was to be the increasing problem of horse thieves along the United States border, the worst of those thieves being a band of men known as the McGraw Gang. With capable officers such as Charles involved, the thieves were soon captured and most of the horses recovered.

After the dissolution of this law enforcement agency due to Charles's successful tenure, Charles went on to join the Manitoba Provincial Police in Dauphin to continue his duties.

Charles Rooke (Photo Credit: Family of Charles Rooke)

During the regular course of business on January 26, 1913, Constable Rooke was instructed to serve a warrant for the arrest of John Baran for non-support of his wife and children. The job of effecting service of the warrant fell to Const. Rooke not only because others had attempted and failed to accomplish the task, but also because he was a wily veteran, a very successful officer, and had a history with the accused.

John Baran's reputation in the community, and the relationship between him and Const. Rooke, was described in the book *Line of Fire: Heroism, Tragedy, and Canada's Police*, by Edward Butts, as follows:

> *Over the next few years, Constable Rooke won the respect and friend-ship of most of the people in the Dauphin area, many of whom were immigrants from Eastern Europe. Around 1911, however, he began to have trouble with John Baran, a Galician who had homesteaded near Dauphin. Baran was a bully and a lout. He didn't bother to work his land, and if it wasn't for the moose meat he brought home, his wife and children would have starved. Baran was reputed to be skilled at carving things with his hands, but he didn't have enough ambition to make a trade of it. His home was a miserable shack. Even Baran's Galician neighbours despised him.*

Two years prior, Const. Rooke had dealt with the arrest and subse-quent jailing of Baran for spousal abuse. His wife had then left Dauphin with two of their four children. The remaining two still living with Baran soon fell into a severe state of deprivation and starvation. Once again, Rooke intervened, rescuing the children from their dire circumstances in the Baran household and placing them into child protection services.

JOHN BARAN
WHO SHOT CONSTABLE ROOKE.

MRS. JOHN BARAN
DESERTED BY HER HUSBAND.

John Baran and wife (Photo Credit: Dauphin Herald)

Const. Rooke set out on that fateful day in January to begin what would turn out to be the final confrontation between the two men. He travelled by sleigh to attend upon Baran, who was living at the time with Annie Chizyk (a.k.a. Maria Pellock) and a child thought to be his, in a settlement in the Riding Mountain region – 15 miles south of Dauphin. It was thought wise that Mr. John Tomski would accompany Const. Rooke not only because he could drive the sleigh, but he could also converse with Baran in the same Galician language. Rooke and Tomski made their way to the homestead and parked the sleigh at a neighbour's place so they could approach Baran's residence on foot without being noticed.

The devastating, life-changing events that played out that day are described in great detail in the *Line of Fire* as follows:

They arrived at the shack at noon, and knocked on the porch door. Annie Chizyk [a woman who was living with Baran] appeared at a window and said Baran was not home.

Knowing Baran from previous encounters, Rooke was sure that the woman was lying. He stepped past Tomski and entered the porch, then started to open the cabin door.

Three bullets smashed through the rough wooden door. Two whistled harmlessly away, but the third struck Rooke in the chest, just above the heart. Startled though he was, Tomski dragged Rooke off the porch and away from the cabin. He had to leave the constable on the ground while he ran to the nearest farm for assistance.

The farmer helped Tomski carry Rooke back to his house. Tomski then drove nine miles to the nearest house with a telephone and called the police station in Dauphin. A doctor hurried to the farmhouse in a sleigh

and saw that there was little he could do for the wounded man there. He wrapped Rooke in blankets, put him in his sleigh, and took him to the little Dauphin hospital.

The book goes on to describe what happened after the shooting, with further tragic results:

Meanwhile, the police in Dauphin organized a six-man posse. They also called MPP headquarters in Winnipeg. Deputy Commissioner John McKenzie and Detective John Parr headed for Dauphin. Before they arrived, the posse set out for the Baran homestead. The shadow of tragedy was about to grow darker.

On the morning of January 27, the posse cautiously approached Baran's cabin. There did not seem to be anybody around. Suddenly there was a roar as flashes of gunfire came from the window. The posse responded with a volley of bullets, riddling the small cabin. Then they waited.

Once the shootout ended, and the last bullet landed, the resulting tragedy unfolded before their eyes. Upon entering the cabin, the posse saw Annie Chizyk laying on the floor, bleeding from gunshot wounds to the chest and waist. And then the shocking revelation of the baby boy, lying dead on the bed, having been hit by a stray bullet. Baran had escaped. While the posse returned to Dauphin with the injured woman and deceased child, the MPP officers McKenzie and Parr set out to track Baran, quickly locating him five miles from his cabin.

Once in custody, Baran blamed the shooting of Const. Rooke on Annie Chizyk – a story which Annie initially corroborated, but later admitted she had lied because of her fear of Baran.

The status of Const. Rooke's condition was reported in the *Dauphin Herald* on January 30, 1913:

Constable Rooke Shot – CONDITION CRITICAL

Thursday, Jan. 30th, 11:30 a.m. – Constable Rooke's condition critical, but he is holding his own well considering the wound is of such a danger-ous character.

An inquest into the death of the baby was convened and reported in the newspaper on the same date of January 30, 1913:

THE INQUEST

The inquest on the death of the Baran baby, who was shot Monday by the police posse which went to the Galician settlement, was held, on Tuesday in the town hall. Evidence was taken from Dr. Ross, Chief of Police Bridle, F. May, W. Evans, W. Knight, E. Turland and Fred Little, members of the posse who did the shooting. The evidence produced showed that the child was killed almost instantly, the bullet passing through the body, causing a shock and hemorrhage.

…

After viewing the remains of the child and hearing the evidence, they returned the following verdict:

VERDICT OF JURY

We, the jury empaneled to take evidence as to the death of the baby Baran, on Jan. 27th, find that the baby came to his death by being shot with a rifle in the hands of one of the posse under Chief Bridle, organized for the purpose of arresting John Baran, suspected of having shot Constable Rooke, and the death of the baby, while regrettable, was purely accidental under the circumstances and we attach no blame to any member of the posse.

With respect to the condition of Annie Chizyk, who had been shot during the raid and was being blamed for the shooting of Const. Rooke, it was reported as follows:

1913 Jan 30 – Woman Placed Under Arrest

Annie Chisyk, who is a patient in the hospital suffering from a bullet wound, was formally placed under arrest on Wednesday, charged with shooting Constable Rooke. Her trial was set for Feb. 4th.

Const. Rooke held on from his injuries as long as he could, but finally passed away. His death was reported in *The Winnipeg Tribune* on February 3, 1913:

BARAN TO BE ACCUSED OF MURDER

Constable Charles Rooke Succumbed to Bullet Wound in Dauphin This Morning.

Constable C. Rooke passed away this morning at ten minutes to seven, eight days almost to the minute since receiving the wound from a rifle fired from the house of John Baran, the Galician whom he was endeavoring to arrest on a charge of non-support.

Little Hope From First

Very little hope was held out by Dr. Harrington, who attended him, but Mr. Rooke had a very rugged constitution, which coupled with a strong will-power, and a determination to get better served him in good stead, and enabled him to conserve his strength much longer than was hoped for.

He had a private day and night nurse, and everything possible was done, but the bullet wound proved too much for human skill to cope with.

. . .

An ante-mortem statement is to be taken from the Chenshi woman, who was living with Baran and who claims to have been the person who shot Constable Rooke. She, it is believed, will succumb to the wound sustained in her battle with the posse.

A charge of murder will be preferred against Baran.

Hon. J.H. Howden, attorney-general, this morning expressed his regret at Constable Rooke's death, and said he was considered one of the best officers in the service.

R.B. Graham, deputy attorney-general, and Chief Elliott also expressed their regret, and said they felt his loss keenly as a personal friend, and as an officer of the department.

February 3, 1913, was a tragic day: the death of Const. Rooke occurred; John Baran was charged with his murder; and, a Coroner's inquest was held. The day's events were reported in the February 6, 1913, edition of the *Dauphin Herald*:

1913 Feb 6 – Baran Fired Fatal Shot

…

Witnesses examined were Dr. Culbertson, as to immediate cause of death; John Tomaski, the man who drive the sleigh that carried Constable Rooke to Baran's house where he was shot, and Marie Pelech, the woman who lived with Baran. The jury, in order to receive the woman's evidence, proceeded to the hospital and for an hour listened to a well connected and intelligent reciting of the incidents which led up to the shooting.

The woman testified that Baran fired two shots from a rifle through the door when Rooke attempted to force an entrance; that she knew that one of the bullets took effect for she examined the spot where Rooke fell exhausted in the snow, when the man who accompanied him left to secure assistance. She stated that she found a pool of blood. She also testified that Baran forced her to state that she fired two shot(s) through the door. The whole affair was brought home to Baran in a most vivid manner.

The jury of the Coroner's inquest came back with the following verdict:

We, the jury empanelled to hear the evidence as to the death of Provincial Constable Charles Rooke, find that the said Charles Rooke on Sunday, Jan. 26, 1913, received a bullet in the breast from a rifle in the hands of John Baran and that the said Charles Rooke died on Monday, Feb. 3, 1913, from the effects of this shot.

The impact of the incident was reported in that same edition of the newspaper:

The death of Constable Rooke has cast a gloom over the community as he was a good citizen, as well a good officer, unassuming and kind to all.

Marie Pelech, who lived with Baran, is still in the hospital, but is doing as well as can be expected. If she recovers she will have to have her right arm amputated at the shoulder. Her brother, Michael, arrived from Winnipeg Monday morning and was overcome with grief to find his sister in such a pitiable condition. He says he has been looking for her for three years.

As to the fate of John Baran:

Baran appeared before Police Magistrate Munson on Monday on the charge of murder. He was remanded until Friday for trial.

The preliminary hearing for John Baran was conducted and reported in the *Dauphin Herald*:

1913 Feb 13 – Baran Committed For Murder

The adjourned preliminary trial of John Baran, under arrest for the murder of Constable Rooke, was concluded on Saturday. Magistrate Munson remanded the prisoner to Portage la Prairie, to stand his trial at the next criminal court on a charge of murder.

The court was called to order at eleven o'clock, the court house being crowded by a throng who were anxious to hear the outcome of the trial.

The prisoner had to be assisted into the court by two officers and appeared in a very weak condition. Later he fell from his chair to the floor, where he was allowed to lie during the trial.

Dr. Harrington gave evidence as to his attendance on Constable Rooke, and stated death to have been caused by the bullet wound, and resultant weakness.

*When the charge was read the prisoner declined to make any statement.
Bertram Ryan, for the defence, admitted that Baran had fired the shot
which killed Constable Rooke, but pleaded justification on a plea of
provocation, claiming Baran could not have known it was an officer of
the law who was demanding entrance and then breaking in the door
of his house, and that Baran had a right to defend his home and had
fired the shot with the intention only of frightening away whoever was
forcing his door. He asked to have the charge at least modified to one
of manslaughter.*

*In passing sentence, Magistrate Munson severely criticized the past
character of the prisoner and had no hesitation in committing him on a
charge of murder to stand his trial at the Portage spring assizes.*

John Baran entered his plea in court, as was reported in the
Dauphin Herald:

1913 Mar 6 – Baran Pleads Not Guilty

*The assizes opened on Tuesday at Portage la Prairie. The Baran case is
the most important one on the docket. Contrary to expectations Baran
has put in a plea of 'not guilty.' The witnesses from here are Mary Peleck,
the woman who was in the house at the time the shot was fired, E.A.
Munson, S.A. McLean, J. Tomoski, A. Rzesnoski and Dr. Harrington.*

THE TRIAL

The trial of John Baran was held on March 6 and 7, 1913, with Judge
Prendergast presiding. It took only one hour and forty minutes for the jury
to render their guilty verdict. When the time came for sentencing, despite
the confession of Baran to the shooting of Rooke, the Judge showed no
mercy, handing down the maximum penalty – the death sentence. The
Judge advised Baran not to hold out hope for a pardon or commuting of

his death sentence and told him to make peace with his God. The hanging was scheduled for May 20, 1913, at 8:00 a.m.

Once convicted and sentenced, the newspaper reported how Baran was spending his last few months alive:

1913 Mar 20 – Baran Now Praying

John Baran, condemned to be hanged for the murder of Constable Rooke, now spends his time in prayer.

Just a few days before Baran's hanging, the necessary preparations were being made, as detailed in the *Dauphin Herald*:

1913 May 15 – Baran to Hang on Tuesday

A Portage la Prairie dispatch says: All hope of reprieve for John Baran under sentence of death for the murder of Constable Rooke, has been given up, and preparations will be started the latter part of the week for the carrying out of the sentence that he be hanged on Tuesday, May 20. Portage is without a sheriff and for that reason none of the new officials are to discuss the matter, but the duty will probably devolve on George Muir, the duty sheriff although he has yet received no definite instructions to prepare to carrying out the death sentence. It is known, however that the gallows will be erected in the jail yard the latter part of this week, and it is understood that a government official will arrive about Saturday to superintendent this week. Portage has never had a hanging and the official(s) are not versed in what is really necessary.

One can only imagine the excitement and curiosity in Portage la Prairie when the preparations began for the first execution in the community. By today's standards, witnessing a hanging would be considered unthinkable, horrific, and macabre, to say the least. Back in 1913, however, a great many people were very interested in seeing and participating in the spectacle. In fact, on the eve of the execution, a constant flow of residents was allowed permission to get a preliminary view of the gallows.

The day of reckoning for John Baran arrived on May 20, 1913. His last moments were recorded in graphic detail in the May 22 edition of the *Dauphin Herald*:

> *Portage la Prairie, May 20 – John Baran at one minute past eight o'clock this morning paid the death penalty in the yard of the Portage la Prairie jail for the murder of Constable Rooke. He walked to his death without even an expression of regret for his deed, and three-quarters of an hour after the drop on the scaffold he was buried in the corner of the jail yard in quick lime, no friends having made claim to his body. Baran spent a sleepless night, dozing off for a few minutes at a time, and at 7:30 this morning asked for his breakfast, which consisted of porridge, eggs, toast and coffee. He did not eat it with a relish and was left quietly alone for his last meal. It was just 7:55 when Deputy Sheriff Muir read the death warrant to the condemned man, and preparations for the march to the scaffold was then begun.*

In the article "*The Forgotten Policeman*" by Staff Sergeant Jack Templeman, the final moments of John Baran's life are recounted:

> *Baran was comforted during his last night by Bishop Boudka of the Ruthenian Church. He was left alone to eat his last breakfast and at 7:55 a.m. Deputy Sheriff Muir read the death warrant and they began the short walk outside. Captain Sheppard, Governor of the Jail and two guards accompanied the prisoner. Turnkey Gordon of Portage was assisted by Turnkey Handel from Winnipeg. Handel is reported to have told Baran to 'brace up and be a man' after which he walked to the gallows with a firm step.*

Hangman Arthur Ellis moved quickly and efficiently when Baran appeared at 8:00 a.m. and within a minute the straps and hood were in place and the trap doors sprung open to drop him 7 feet breaking his neck instantly. The newspapers reported that Hangman Ellis was satisfied that the execution was conducted in a most credible manner. Mr. Ellis does not conceal his identity, but he does go about heavily armed. After the body was cut down an Inquest was held and he took this opportune time to go out for breakfast and was able to return in time to be present for the burial. It was reported that Mr. Ellis travels next to Prince Albert where two more executions are scheduled soon.

The Inquest concluded that death was the result of hanging by order of the court and the body was then removed for burial in the courtyard. A wooden coffin built in the jail was lined with quicklime and the body placed inside. It was then covered with more quicklime and the lid nailed shut. It was buried in the south-west corner of the yard only 45 minutes after the execution.

THE EXECUTIONER

The executioner brought in to conduct the hanging of John Baran was the best in the land – Canada's most well-known and experienced hangman, Mr. Arthur Ellis. (While his real name was Arthur English, he took on the alias Arthur Ellis, likely inspired by the English hangman John Ellis.) Mr. Ellis was hired by the federal government in about 1913 to become the official executioner of the Dominion of Canada, travelling across the country performing hangings.

Performing a successful hanging was not a simple one. The goal was to break the neck as quickly as possible so that death would come relatively quickly and painlessly. Many calculations needed to be done and factors taken into consideration: the length of rope depended on the victim's weight, the thickness of a person's neck, the springiness of the gallows beam, and the stretch of the rope.

Ellis took his job seriously and in 1915 set a new record for the speed of a hanging when he executed Dutch Wagner in 47 seconds. Over the next two decades his speed increased several times, with one execution taking a mere 15 seconds.

On March 29, 1935, Ellis, at the age of 71, was called upon once more, this time to perform the execution of Tomasina Teolis who had been convicted of plotting to kill her husband. Ellis made his usual calculations for the length of the rope required based on Teolis's weight. However, despite his years of experience, he failed to notice that while incarcerated she had gained 42 pounds and the necessary adjustments to shorten the rope were not done. As a result, when Teolis fell through trapdoor of the gallows, the noose sprang back up empty – Tomasina Teolis had been decapitated.

As the hanging of a woman was not looked upon favourably, and due to the unfortunate circumstances of his last execution, the career of Canada's hangman came to an end – a career that had carried out over 600 hangings in Canada, Britain, and the Middle East.

For 20 years Ellis had been so successful in hiding his true profession from friends and relatives that even his wife was unaware and believed he was a government public servant who travelled a lot on business. Upon discovering the truth, she was so horrified she left him and refused to live with him again. Three years after the botched hanging and having fallen into a life of poverty in Montreal, he died from starvation on July 21, 1938.

SACRIFICE

A routine call to serve a warrant had gone horribly wrong and the lives of many were changed that day. One man was dead, another hanged, a woman was left permanently disfigured, and a child's short life was ended.

Charles Rooke, the immigrant from England who had come to Canada with great hopes and dreams, paid the ultimate price in fulfilling his duty and enforcing the laws of this land. He was 36 years old and left behind a wife and two young children. He was buried in Riverside Cemetery, Dauphin, Manitoba, and the Masonic Lodge erected the headstone.

Charles Rooke headstone, Dauphin (Photo Credit: John Burchill)

While his body remains in Canada, back home in England he was memorialized on his father Benjamin's headstone in Reigate, Surrey.

Charles Rooke memorialized on headstone, England
(Photo Credit: billiongraves.com – Rick Powell)

(Transcription: Loving memory of: Benjamin Proctor Rooke, M.D., late of the Bombay Medical Department, who died Oct. 8, 1887, aged 86, Also Charles, youngest son of the above, who died 3rd Feb. 1913, at Dauphin from result of wounds while on duty with Manitoba Mounted Police, aged 36.)

As a tribute to Charles, and in recognition of the 150th Anniversary of the Manitoba Provincial Police in 2020, a lake was named after him. Charles Rooke Lake was officially dedicated on November 20, 2020, and is located at 52.695133 latitude and -99.353277 longitude in the Interlake region of central Manitoba, 178 kilometers north east of Dauphin. Charles Rooke also has a place of honour in Canada, being listed as one of Canada's fallen officers on the Canadian Police and Peace Officers Memorial located in Ottawa.

Canadian Police & Peace Officers Memorial, Ottawa
(Photo Credit: cppom.ca)

Memorial panel noting Charles Rooke (Photo Credit: Stephen Boucher)

PART 3:
Epilogue

EPILOGUE

MARK TWAIN, IN HIS 1897 travel book entitled *Following the Equator: A Journey Around the World*, reinterpreted and expanded on the phrase "Truth is stranger than fiction" by adding that "Fiction is obliged to stick to possibilities; Truth isn't". A fictitious story could not be written with a more flamboyant cast of characters than in this family. It is hard to imagine anyone dreaming up such a grand story that included a lawyer turned mayor of a small British village, a physician to a British queen, a father who raised a future Hawaiian queen, a gentleman who lived an unconventional communal lifestyle, a man who socialized with an empress, a family wiped out by a tragedy at sea, and a murder with a subsequent hanging. And yet this is not fiction!

"Don't judge a book by its cover". That saying could not be more relevant and appropriate than in Aubrey Rooke's case. At the age of 16, this English boy came to Canada due to a terminal diagnosis. Taking up residence in a small shack in the rolling hills of the Fort Qu'Appelle valley, he lived a quiet, modest life. One would never have suspected that such an unassuming man had come from an aristocratic, refined background and was heir to a fortune. Aubrey Rooke chose to live a different way of life than that of his family – not one of prestige, status or elegance, and yet still extraordinary. He lived among the Indigenous people, befriended them, and tried to make a difference in their lives; took a leadership role in his community by volunteering in a national election; and, through an Act of the Canadian Parliament, attempted to construct a rail line to improve the lives of his fellow citizens. Despite his simple, meager lifestyle, he nonetheless made a significant impact on the people he came in contact with and provided a major contribution to the vibrancy, development, and progress of his community.

With their adventurous spirits and non-conformist lifestyles, the remarkable members of the Rooke family left behind a legacy of historical significance. However, this is also a family that time has forgotten. Now that their story has been told, their voices are heard once more and, in a way, they live again.

LIST OF SOURCES

A History of the Indian Medical Service, 1600-1913, Vol. II.

Acts of the Parliament of the Dominion of Canada, 1 Edward VII, May 23, 1901, Chapter 58.

Butts, Edward, *Line of Fire: Heroism, Tragedy, and Canada's Police.*

Calgary Herald, August 18, 1934, *Canadian Press* article "Naming of Qu'Appelle Legend Is Denied by 64-Year-old Englishman".

Canadian Census Return – 1901.

Canadian Census Return – 1906.

Canadian Census Return – 1911.

Canadian Census Return – 1916.

Canadian Census Return – 1921.

Canadian Census Return – 1926.

Dauphin Herald, January 30, 1913, "Constable Rooke Shot".

Dauphin Herald, February 6, 1913, "Baran Fired Fatal Shot".

Dauphin Herald, February 13, 1913, "Baran Committed for Murder".

Dauphin Herald, March 6, 1913, "Baran Pleads Not Guilty".

Dauphin Herald, March 20, 1913, "Baran Now Praying".

Dauphin Herald, May 15, 1913, "Baran to Hang on Tuesday".

Dauphin Herald, May 22, 1913, "Portage la Prairie".

Dominion Elections Act, 1900 (S.C. 1900, c.12) (s.51).

Dominion Elections Act, 1900 (S.C. 1900, c.12) (s.147), (para. 19).

Dominion Elections Act, 1900 (S.C. 1900, c.12) (s.147), (para. 27).

Greer, Richard A., 1969 article, "The Founding of the Queen's Hospital".

Honolulu Star-Bulletin, "Tales About Hawaii", December 16, 1955, referenced in the Hawaii Medical Journal.

Last Will and Testament of Cresswell Keane Charles Rooke, dated April 17, 1902.

Last Will and Testament of Emma Kaleleonalani (Queen Emma), dated October 21, 1884.

Last Will and Testament of Thomas Charles Byde Rooke, dated February 28, 1852.

Letter from Cresswell Paillet Rooke to Ernest Greatorex, dated December 8, 1962.

"Oceana" and "Pisagua", The Merchant Shipping Act, 1894, (No. 7539), decision dated June 25, 1912.

Official Report of the Debates of the House of Commons of the Dominion of Canada, First Session-Ninth Parliament, 1 Edward VII, 1901, held April 29, 1901.

Papers of the Hawaiian Historical Society, Number 17, September 30, 1930.

Regina Leader-Post article March 17, 1937, "For Half Century Rooke Counsellor To Valley Indians".

Regina Leader-Post, December 12, 1940, article "A Certain Man Had Two Sons" by W.A. Cameron.

Rooke v. Queen's Hospital, 12 Haw. 375 (1900).

Rural Preliminary List of Electors – 1940.

Rural Preliminary List of Electors – 1945.

Rural Preliminary List of Electors – 1949.

Rural Preliminary List of Electors – 1953.

Rural Preliminary List of Electors – 1957.

Templeman, Staff Sergeant Jack, article "The Forgotten Policeman".

The Evening Bulletin, March 16, 1901, "Valuable Property Was Sold Today."

The Hawaiian Journal of History, vol. 22 (1988), article by Rhoda E.A. Hackler, "My Dear Friend: Letters of Queen Victoria and Queen Emma".

The Hawaiian Star, October 4, 1897, "An Important Case".

The Hawaiian Star, October 5, 1897, "Half A Million Involved".

The Hawaiian Star, November 30, 1898, "Queen's Hospital Loses".

The Hawaiian Star, May 11, 1900, "Queen's Hospital Loses. Stripped of Property By The Supreme Court".

The Hawaiian Star, May 14, 1900, "Other Parties Affected. Interested in the Queen's Hospital Case".

The Hawaiian Star, October 9, 1908, "Magoon's Fat Fee".

The Independent, March 16, 1901, "Important Land Sale".

The Pacific Commercial Advertiser, May 15, 1900, "Rooke Decision is Far Reaching".

The Pacific Commercial Advertiser, May 17, 1900, "Rooke Decision Has Aftermath".

The Pacific Commercial Advertiser, December 12, 1900, "Day of the Outbreak".

The Pacific Commercial Advertiser, February 12, 1901, "Land of Rooke. Valuable Property To Be Vended at Auction".

The Pacific Commercial Advertiser, April 26, 1903, "Society".

The Pacific Commercial Advertiser, June 21, 1903, "Society."

The Pacific Commercial Advertiser, March 26, 1904, "Victoria's Gift To Queen Emma To Leave Hawaii".

The Polynesian, December 11, 1858.

The Winnipeg Tribune, February 3, 1913, "Baran To Be Accused of Murder".

Twain, Mark, 1897 travel book, *Following the Equator: A Journey Around the World.*

Winnipeg Free Press, June 25, 1927, article "People of Old Fort Qu'Appelle" by William Bleasdell Cameron.

CPSIA information can be obtained
at www.ICGtesting.com
Printed in the USA
BVHW060445150322
631474BV00003B/16